SINFULLY EASY
DELICIOUS DESSERTS

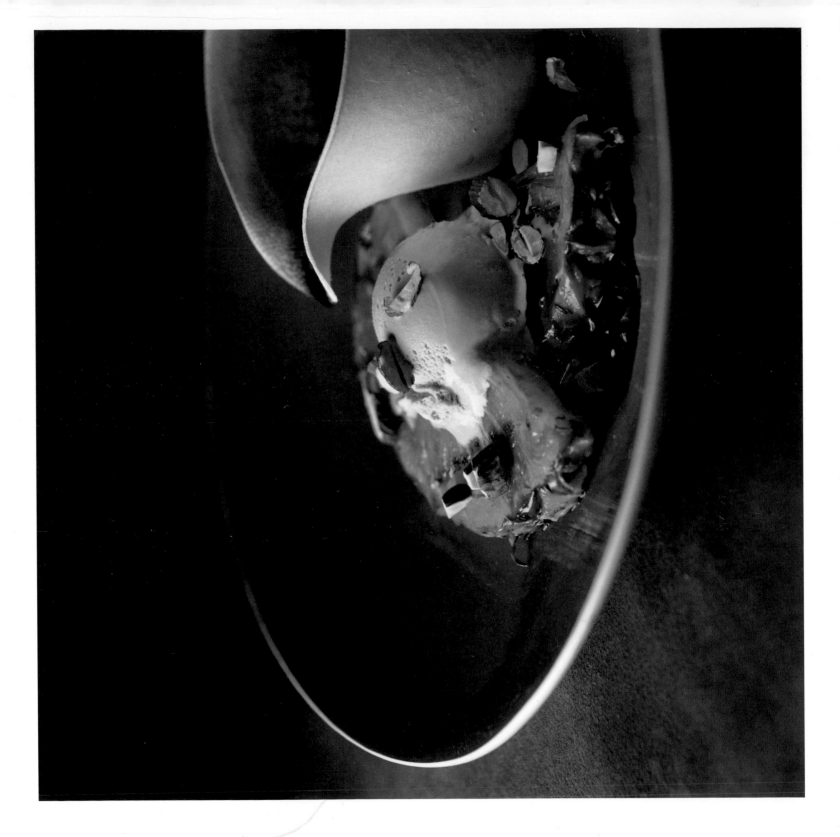

SINFULLY EASY
DELICIOUS DESSERTS

ALICE MEDRICH

PHOTOGRAPHS
BY SANG AN

ARTISAN

ALSO BY ALICE MEDRICH

CHEWY GOOEY CRISPY CRUNCHY MELT-IN-YOUR-MOUTH COOKIES

PURE DESSERT

CHOCOLATE HOLIDAYS: UNFORGETTABLE DESSERTS FOR EVERY SEASON

BITTERSWEET: RECIPES AND TALES FROM A LIFE IN CHOCOLATE

ALICE MEDRICH'S COOKIES AND BROWNIES

CHOCOLATE AND THE ART OF LOW-FAT DESSERTS

COCOLAT: EXTRAORDINARY CHOCOLATE DESSERTS

Published by Artisan
A division of Workman Publishing Company, Inc.
225 Varick Street
New York, NY 10014-4381
www.artisanbooks.com

Published simultaneously in Canada by Thomas Allen & Son, Limited

Library of Congress Cataloging-in-Publication Data
Medrich, Alice.
Sinfully easy delicious desserts : Alice Medrich.
    p. cm.
Includes index.
ISBN 978-1-57965-398-9
1. Desserts. I. Title.
TX773.M4278 2012
641.86—dc23   2011035405

Design by Morla Design
Art direction and styling by Sara Slavin
Food styling by Sandra Cook

Printed in China
First printing, May 2012

10 9 8 7 6 5 4 3 2 1

FOR LUCY

CONTENTS

INTRODUCTION

The inspiration for this book dates back in part to my own pre-pastry chef days. A dessert I ate in a very modest neighborhood café in Paris in the early '70s gave me the seed of an idea that has percolated in the back of my mind ever since. The dessert was simply a big scoop of sweetened chestnut puree (right out of the can) topped with a generous dollop of thick, tart, nutty-tasting crème fraîche (right out of the carton). My idea was certainly not to make a book of desserts from the contents of cans and cartons; but it was the notion that desserts could be delicious, sophisticated, or subtle—even luxurious, rich, and decadent—without being complicated. Good desserts could be simple and require little skill or time to prepare, just the knowledge or awareness that two or three elements taste divine together.

Over the years I've encountered more "sinfully easy" desserts in the homes of friends, usually busy people who are confident in the kitchen but more comfortable preparing savory dishes than preparing sweets. Regardless, they have a discerning eye for choosing recipes or putting elements together with panache. None are skilled dessert makers, but all are marvelous hosts.

My sinfully easy desserts are a snap to put together, forgiving, and flexible, with a focus on flavor. They also lend themselves to creative thinking and variations. Many of them rely on the usual sound judgment and taste-and-adjust habits of good cooks rather than on the pastry chef's patience, precise measuring habits, and trust in the chemistry of the recipe. Some of these recipes make use of convenient pantry items, such as special preserves or honey, frozen fruit, nut butters, etc. And some even involve simple but foolproof baking.

These are recipes that will become part of your repertoire; from them you will choose your rabbits-from-hats, your effortless signature desserts. Some are so easy to do that they don't even need a proper recipe, just a short description. Some of them are assembled, like a good salad, with flavors and textures juxtaposed in a flexible and intuitive way. Many you can remember by heart. But all require fewer steps, less equipment, less measuring, less precision, less fuss.

Sinfully Easy Delicious Desserts offers a change of pace from complex and competitive TV cooking or the restaurant pastry chef's high-wire act. It's a little push back against the idea that desserts need to be complicated or demand skills that most people don't have, a collection of recipes with a focus on flavor, texture, and pleasure: simplicity at the very highest level.

THE DESSERT MAKER'S BASIC PANTRY

Having these staples on hand means you can whip up most of the desserts in this book on the spur of the moment.

IN THE PANTRY

Unbleached all-purpose flour

Granulated sugar

Brown sugar: light and/or dark

Baking powder

Baking soda

Salt

Cornstarch

Chocolate of all kinds, including chocolate chips

Cocoa powder: natural and/or Dutch-process

Spices: cinnamon sticks, ground cinnamon, whole nutmeg, ground and/or whole cardamom pods, ground cloves, ground allspice, aniseeds, black pepper (preferably whole peppercorns, in a grinder)

Pure vanilla extract

Pure almond extract

Peanut butter and almond or other nut butters

Dried fruit: raisins and/or currants, cherries, pears, apricots, dates

Crystallized (candied) ginger

Nuts: almonds, walnuts, hazelnuts (filberts), peanuts, pistachios, pecans

Unsulphured (but not blackstrap) molasses

IN THE FREEZER

Vanilla ice cream

Fresh lemon juice and/or lime juice (squeeze the juice after you've zested the peel, freeze in an ice cube tray, and then bag the juice cubes)

Pineapple juice concentrate

IN THE FRIDGE

Milk

Cream (pasteurized cream has a better flavor, but ultra-pasteurized cream keeps well for a long time)

Unsalted butter

Sour cream

Eggs

Plain yogurt: Greek and/or regular

Lemons and limes

Apples

Oranges

✳ GOOD TO KNOW

With your basic pantry, here are just a few of the quickest desserts you can make without reaching for your shopping bag and car keys.

Almond Cake (page 202)

Apples in Cardamom Lime Syrup (page 50)

The Best One-Bowl Chocolate Cake (page 174)

Bittersweet Brownie Drops (page 248)

Cocoa Brownies with Walnuts and Brown Butter (page 251)

Honey Balsamic Sundaes (page 16)

Maya's Lemon-Scented Apple Upside-Down Cake (page 69)

My Chocolate Pudding 3.0 (page 88)

Pantry Gingerbread (page 213)

Queen of Sheba Torte 5.0 (page 183)

Right-Brain Nutty Butter Cookies (page 238)

Sour Cream Soufflés (page 123)

And don't miss the ideas on page 22, Things to Do with Vanilla Ice Cream.

7 THINGS GREAT TO HAVE

See the Equipment section on page 274 for a complete list, but here are the seven things you may not have that will make your dessert-preparing life easier.

1] **STRAINERS** Use small fine-mesh strainers for dusting a dessert with powdered sugar and straining cooked mixtures that contain eggs, such as custards. A large medium-fine-mesh strainer takes the place of a flour sifter; it's easier to use and easier to clean. These are useful for savory cooking too. Inexpensive strainers are fine.

2] **SILICONE SPATULAS** Nothing beats these heatproof spatulas, the modern version of the rubber spatula. They don't melt or crack, so you can use them for stovetop cooking where you might ordinarily use a wooden spoon, and they are shaped better for sweeping the sides, bottoms, and corners of pots to prevent things from sticking or burning. They are especially useful for making custards and puddings.

3] **STAINLESS STEEL BOWLS** Stainless steel bowls heat up and cool down quickly, making them especially useful for melting chocolate or for anything else you do in a water bath or an improvised double boiler. No need to buy the most expensive ones.

4] **STAINLESS STEEL WIRE WHISKS** The most useful shape is long and narrow, rather than round or balloon shaped, as a long, narrow whisk can reach into and sweep the corners of a saucepan. You can also whip cream with it.

5] **INSTANT-READ THERMOMETER** Instant-read thermometers are easier to read and register the temperature faster than dial thermometers, and you need fast when cooking some egg-based mixtures. Bonus: these are great for testing the doneness of roasted meats and poultry, their original purpose.

6] **MICROPLANE ZESTER** This simple but elegantly designed tool gives us an effortless (and rather stylish) way to grate citrus zest into batters, or to shower a little fragrance—finely grated cinnamon stick or nutmeg—over a serving of dessert.

7] **9½-INCH FLUTED TART PAN WITH A REMOVABLE BOTTOM** It may seem kind of fancy and French, but get one of these lovely-to-look-at and easy-to-use pans and you will pull it out often to make the simple tarts in this book and any other tarts from the classic baking repertoire. Really.

✳ **GOOD TO KNOW**

Don't feel you have to buy the heaviest or most expensive bowls, whisks, or strainers.

Take a deep breath and toss out that handful of stained and deteriorated rubber spatulas, those ancient wooden spoons, and your seldom-used sifter.

MAGIC INGREDIENTS

These are the ingredients I keep on hand to transform a bowl of oranges into dessert, turn chocolate pudding into company fare, or elevate any number of good things.

BLACK PEPPERCORNS, whole, in a grinder. Pass the pepper grinder when you serve ripe figs with fresh cheese and honey, or strawberries with a splash of balsamic vinegar, or even a chocolate mousse.

FLAKY SEA SALT A tiny pinch of flaky sea salt lifts a dish of chocolate mousse or ice cream with caramel sauce, or the olive oil drizzled over ice cream.

ORANGE BLOSSOM WATER A few drops sprinkled over orange slices turns them into dessert. Or add to whipped cream along with a little grated orange zest to top a chocolate dessert.

ROSE WATER With a drop or two, flavor sweetened whipped cream to serve with strawberries and/or raspberries or cubes of watermelon. Toss sugared strawberries with a few drops.

CINNAMON STICKS Use a Microplane zester to grate a little cinnamon over any dark chocolate dessert, from brownies to chocolate chip cookies to chocolate pudding. Grate over the whipped cream topping on a chocolate or fruit dessert. Grate over orange slices, peach or nectarine slices, or a fruit salad. Or grate over rice pudding or over cocoa-dusted chocolate truffles just before serving.

WHOLE NUTMEG Grate over brownies just before serving, or over the whipped cream topping on any chocolate or fruit dessert, or over rice pudding.

FORTIFIED WINES (such as sherry, port, Marsala, Madeira, or Banyuls). Macerate berries or sliced stone fruit for up to 2 hours before serving plain or with ice cream or cream. Reduce by half and chill, then pour an ounce or so over a scoop of ice cream in an old-fashioned glass, and top off with soda water for a delicious float or soda.

SPIRITS AND LIQUEURS (such as rum, brandy, whiskey, kirsch, framboise, poire Williams, amaretto, Grand Marnier, Frangelico, etc.). Toss with fruit, splash on cakes, pour over ice cream, or use for dunking amaretti.

LIMES Grate the zest over sliced fruit and then drizzle with the juice. Grate the zest over a bowl of cocoa-dusted truffles along with freshly grated cinnamon just before serving. Grate the zest over warm gingerbread.

HONEY Drizzle over yogurt or ricotta cheese, perhaps topped with pistachios, walnuts, or toasted almonds, or over vanilla ice cream. Drizzle over slices of ripe melon and garnish with ricotta and torn basil leaves. Drizzle (especially chestnut honey) over Gorgonzola dolcelatte.

CHOCOLATE See 8 Ideas for a Bar of Chocolate, page 262, for some of my favorite ideas.

JAMS AND PRESERVES Top ricotta cheese or Greek yogurt with a spoonful, smear over crepes before folding them, sandwich with Right-Brain Nutty Butter Cookies (page 238), or make a layer cake with berries and cream (page 229).

SPECIAL SUGARS (muscovado, especially dark, and piloncillo). Eat with sour cream and strawberries. Or simmer with cream to make a quick toffee sauce (see page 25).

EXTRA VIRGIN OLIVE OIL Not just for salads anymore. Drizzle extra virgin olive oil over vanilla ice cream with a sprinkle of flaky salt, or over store-bought almond or hazelnut biscotti. Or use it to make a chocolate torte (page 185), pound cake (page 199), dessert croutons (page 29), or crostini (page 16).

STARTING WITH ICE CREAM

Some of my best desserts begin quietly, with a purchased pint of vanilla (or chocolate, or coffee, or coconut) ice cream. I leave the ice cream maker in the cupboard and spend my scarce dessert-making minutes concocting sensuous sauces and crunchy, craveable toppings. Ice cream desserts are all about the play of flavors, textures, and temperatures. It's easy to imagine cold, creamy ice cream melting against hot dark chocolate sauce, salty silken caramel, or tart warm berries. But ice cream gets exciting with exotic partners: honey and balsamic vinegar with olive oil and strawberries; foamy bitter stout beer and Kahlúa; juicy oranges with dates and almonds; or spicy buttered toast. Sauces and "accessories" are quick to make, and they far surpass any that come in jars or packages. The few made-from-scratch ice creams, sherbets, and granitas in this chapter are irresistible for their ease (none requires an ice cream machine), exceptional flavor, and uniqueness. You'll find summer-fruit ice creams to make when fresh fruit is abundant, and ultrapineappley ice cream (made with frozen concentrate) for when it's scarce. You'll also find a great super-easy lemon sherbet, along with classic icy granitas like lemon and coffee and exciting new ones inspired by Thai iced tea and Vietnamese coffee.

HONEY BALSAMIC SUNDAES

Very chic and sophisticated, and almost effortless. The combination of vanilla ice cream and sauce alone is spectacular; the berries or figs are extra nice. And I *love* the olive oil. If your crowd is adventurous, pass a cruet and let your guests drizzle some over the sundaes and/or serve the sundaes with Olive Oil Crostini. (Photograph on page 14)

Serves 4

INGREDIENTS

FOR THE HONEY BALSAMIC SAUCE

⅔ cup balsamic vinegar (the inexpensive kind is fine)

⅓ cup flavorful but mild honey (such as clover, sage, or orange blossom), or more to taste

4 scoops vanilla ice cream

A carton of ripe strawberries, rinsed, hulled, and halved or quartered, or figs, halved or quartered (optional)

Extra virgin olive oil (optional)

Olive Oil Crostini (optional)

DIRECTIONS

TO MAKE THE SAUCE Combine the vinegar and honey in a small saucepan, bring to a simmer, and simmer until reduced to ½ cup. Let cool.

Taste the sauce with a little of the ice cream and adjust the balance of sweetness with more honey if necessary—though I advise you to keep it fairly tart in contrast with the ice cream. Put a scoop of ice cream in each serving dish, with or without fruit, and drizzle with sauce—it's powerful, so use just a little. (Any leftover sauce can be stored in a covered container in the refrigerator for at least several weeks.) Serve at once. Pass the olive oil separately, if using, and add a couple of crostini, if desired.

✳ VARIATION

Olive Oil Crostini

Toast 8 slices from a regular (not sourdough) baguette in a toaster oven or on a baking sheet in a preheated 350°F oven, turning the slices once, until lightly golden at the edges and perfectly crisp and crunchy. Brush or drizzle the tops liberally with extra virgin olive oil.

FRAGRANT ORANGES WITH ICE CREAM, ALMONDS, AND DATES

Scoops of creamy vanilla ice cream and icy mango sorbet in a pool of juicy scented orange segments with sticky dates, toasted almonds, and a fragrant top note of cinnamon. This combination was inspired by a Moroccan orange salad from Paula Wolfert, the doyenne of Moroccan cooking in America. It's refreshing and light and would especially complement a rich savory meal. For an extra-virtuous dessert or a breakfast or brunch dish, just serve the orange segments with the orange flower water and skip the ice cream, et cetera.

Serves 6

INGREDIENTS

8 oranges

¼ teaspoon orange blossom water, or to taste

6 small scoops vanilla ice cream

6 small scoops mango or orange sorbet

12 plump dates, pitted and quartered

⅓ cup (1.5 ounces) chopped toasted almonds or toasted slivered almonds

A cinnamon stick (optional)

EQUIPMENT

Microplane zester (optional)

DIRECTIONS

UP TO 1 DAY BEFORE SERVING, PREPARE THE ORANGES Segment 6 of the oranges as described in the sidebar or simply peel and slice them, reserving the juices. Pick out any seeds and collect all of the juices and the segments or slices in a bowl.

Continued

✳ **GOOD TO KNOW**

How to Segment an Orange

Cut a generous slice from both ends of the orange to expose a round of bare fruit about 1½ inches in diameter. Set the orange on one cut end on a cutting board. With a sharp knife, starting at the top edge of the rind, use a downward sawing motion, following the contour of the fruit to remove a wide strip of rind, including all the white pith. Continue around the fruit, then trim off any remaining exposed pith on the surface of the fruit.

Hold the orange in a cupped hand over a bowl as you segment it, letting the juices and sections drop into the bowl. Slice between one segment and the membrane, then rotate the knife blade to peel the segment away from the other membrane, or simply cut the segment away from the membrane on both sides.

Cut the remaining 2 oranges in half and juice them. Add the juice to the bowl of oranges. Flavor the oranges delicately with drops of orange flower water to taste. Cover and refrigerate until ready to serve.

To serve, taste the juice and adjust the orange flower water if necessary. Divide the oranges and juices evenly among six serving bowls. Nestle a small scoop of ice cream and a small scoop of sorbet in the center of each bowl. Distribute the quartered dates around the ice cream and sprinkle each dessert with the chopped almonds. Grate a little bit of the cinnamon stick over each bowl, if desired, and serve immediately.

✳ VARIATION

Fragrant Oranges with Ice Cream, Walnuts, and Dates

Substitute rose water for the orange blossom water and raw or toasted walnuts for the toasted almonds.

✳ GOOD TO KNOW

Orange blossom water (and rose water too) is meant to be a beguiling nuance of flavor and fragrance, not a wallop, so use it with a very light hand. Correct the flavoring drop by drop and you can't go wrong.

STOUT FLOATS

An ice cream float made with beer may not be a new idea to craft beer fans and brew pub regulars, but it's too good not to go mainstream. And it's truly a no-brainer to prepare. This is a version with chocolate ice cream and Kahlúa that I enjoyed (loved) at the Creekside Brewing Company in San Luis Obispo a couple of years ago. I make smaller floats in 5- to 6-ounce glasses when I serve them for dessert after a meal.

Serves 6

INGREDIENTS

½ cup Cocoa Syrup (page 24) or store-bought chocolate syrup, chilled

6 tablespoons Kahlúa or other coffee liqueur

6 generous scoops chocolate ice cream

Three 12-ounce bottles (or about 2 pints) stout, chilled

Unsweetened Whipped Cream (page 130), optional

EQUIPMENT

6 tall 10- to 12-ounce glasses

6 straws

6 iced-tea or other long-handled spoons

DIRECTIONS

Pour a tablespoon of cocoa syrup and a tablespoon of coffee liqueur into each glass. Add the scoops of ice cream. Add the stout, pouring it gently down the side of each tilted glass to prevent too much head from forming. Top each float with a dollop of whipped cream, and drizzle with a little more cocoa syrup, if desired. Serve immediately, with the straws and spoons.

✳ VARIATIONS

More Beer Floats

The following special beers, each in its own way, make sensational floats with vanilla ice cream instead of chocolate, and without the chocolate syrup, Kahlúa, or whipped cream:

Franziskaner Hefe-Weisse

Hoegaarden Wit-Blanche (wheat beer)

Maredsous Triple 10 (tripel)

Chimay Blue Cap ale

Maredsous 8 Brune (double)

Samuel Smith's Nut Brown Ale

and finally, delicious but strong and not for the faint of heart:

Spaten Optimator (Doppelbock)

THINGS TO DO WITH VANILLA ICE CREAM

Top with

- Chocolate Sauce "to Taste" (page 23) or Cocoa Fudge Sauce (page 23), with or without sliced strawberries or bananas and whipped cream.

- The Simplest Caramel Sauce (page 25) or Butterscotch Toffee Sauce (page 25) and toasted almonds or hazelnuts or salted peanuts.

- The Simplest Caramel Sauce (page 25) and sprinkle with a pinch of coarse sea salt or crushed cardamom seeds.

- A spoonful of Coffee or Wine or Beer Granita (page 42).

- Bourbon–Brown Sugar Pecans (page 257) and store-bought or homemade caramel sauce (see page 25). Add peach slices, if you like.

- Crushed Praline (page 32) and Saucy Berries (page 81) or Maple Cranberry Sauce (page 80).

Pair with

- Scoops of Pineapple Ice Cream (page 37) or strawberry, orange, mango, or other tangy fruit sorbet.

Drizzle with

- Extra virgin olive oil and sprinkle with a tiny pinch of flaky sea salt. Add Dessert Croutons (page 29) made with extra virgin olive oil, if you like.

Serve on

- Slices of warm toasted pound cake, drizzled with store-bought or home-made caramel sauce (see page 25). Add toasted pecans and/or sliced peaches or nectarines.

- Spice-Drawer Cinnamon Toast (page 28) with any chocolate, cocoa, or cara-mel sauce drizzled over it, or surround with a moat of double-strength hot chocolate or Mexican hot chocolate.

- Baked Hot Chocolate Pudding with the Works (page 99).

- Coconut Meringue (page 166) with or without Chocolate Sauce "to Taste" (page 23) or Cocoa Fudge Sauce (page 23) or on individual Peanut Butter Pavlovas (page 162) garnished with berries.

Serve with

- Cherries with Balsamic Vinegar (page 54) or Vanilla Bean (page 54), Dessert Chutney (page 82), Apples in Cardamom Lime Syrup (page 50), Plums in Brandied Coffee Syrup (page 84), Pears in Ginger Lemon Syrup (page 50), Sautéed Figs (page 49), or Honey–Caramelized Figs (page 56).

Make

- A float with one of the beers listed on page 20 or any other not-too-bitter beer with malty caramel flavors.

- Honey Balsamic Sundaes (page 16).

- Fragrant Oranges with Ice Cream, Almonds, and Dates (page 17).

Sandwich between

- Ultrathin Cocoa Pecan Cookies (page 245) or Ultrathin Chocolate Chunk Cookies (page 243) and drizzle with melted chocolate, Chocolate Sauce "to Taste" (page 23), or Cocoa Fudge Sauce (page 23), or a purchased sauce. Serve with knives and forks.

3 INDISPENSABLE CHOCOLATE SAUCES

Sauce is a reason to lick your lips, dip your fingers, or scrape your plate. Sauce turns the plainest ice cream, cake, or fruit into Dessert with a capital D. When too much is just enough, when gooier is good, when cold needs warm, rich needs bitter, or tart needs sweet, you need a sauce! And you can produce something better than anything store-bought in just minutes. These sauces are fast and fabulous. Keep some in the fridge or freezer. Take them as hostess gifts.

CHOCOLATE SAUCE "TO TASTE"

Once you've made this sauce once or twice, you may do as I do: melt any amount of chocolate you have, then gradually add your chosen liquid, until the sauce is smooth and as thick or thin as you want it to be.

Makes 1¾ to 2 cups

10 ounces bittersweet or semisweet chocolate, finely chopped

½ to 1 cup milk, half-and-half, heavy cream, water, coffee, soy milk, rice milk, or regular or low-fat coconut milk

2 tablespoons (1 ounce) unsalted butter (optional)

½ teaspoon pure vanilla extract or 1 to 3 tablespoons liqueur, such as Grand Marnier, or rum, brandy, or Scotch (optional)

Salt

Put the chocolate and ½ cup milk (or cream, etc.) in a medium heatproof bowl, set it in a wide skillet of barely simmering water, and stir frequently until the chocolate is melted and smooth. Add up to ½ cup more milk if the sauce is too thick, or if it hardens too much when you spoon a little "test" over ice cream. If you are using milk, water, or coffee, taste the sauce and add some or all of the butter if you want to tone down the flavor intensity. Remove the sauce from the heat and stir in the vanilla (or liqueur, etc.) and tiny pinches of salt, to taste. Use immediately, or set the sauce aside then rewarm briefly in a pan of hot water or in the microwave when needed. The sauce keeps in a covered container in the refrigerator for several days, or it can be frozen.

COCOA FUDGE SAUCE (OR FROSTING)

Cocoa Fudge Sauce made with superb cocoa powder has extra-big chocolate flavor. It's divine over ice cream, but it can also be cooled and used to frost a cake or cookies.

Makes about 2 cups

½ cup (1.625 ounces) unsweetened cocoa powder, preferably natural

1 cup (7 ounces) sugar, or more to taste

Pinch of salt, or to taste

1 cup heavy cream

6 tablespoons (3 ounces) unsalted butter, cut into bits

1 teaspoon pure vanilla extract (optional)

Put the cocoa, sugar, and salt in a medium saucepan and stir in just enough of the cream to make a smooth, thick paste, then stir in the rest of the cream. Add the butter and stir over low heat until the butter is melted and the sauce is smooth and hot but not simmering. Taste and add a little more salt and/or sugar, if desired, stirring until it dissolves. Remove from the heat and stir in the vanilla, if using.

Spoon the warm sauce over ice cream, or set aside and then rewarm before using. The sauce keeps in a covered container in the refrigerator for a week, or it can be frozen for up to 3 months. To reheat, put the sauce in a heatproof bowl, set it in a skillet of barely simmering water, and stir occasionally until the sauce is the desired consistency; or microwave on medium (50%) power, using short bursts and stirring frequently.

Continued

To use as a frosting, let cool until spreadable. The recipe makes enough to frost a two-layer cake.

MILK CHOCOLATE SAUCE

You can make this with water, coffee, milk, or cream—richer liquids give the sauce a more luxurious texture, but milder chocolate flavor. Milk chocolate sauce tastes good with ice cream, of course, but also with grilled or sautéed pineapple, or Fresh Ginger Gingerbread (page 213).

Makes I cup

8 ounces milk chocolate

¼ cup plus 2 tablespoons boiling water, hot coffee, or scalded milk or cream

Salt

Chop the chocolate very finely and put it in a bowl. Pour the hot liquid over the chocolate and stir until the chocolate is melted and smooth. Add tiny pinches of salt to taste, if desired. Thin the sauce to the desired consistency with a little water if necessary.

COCOA SYRUP

This flavorful bittersweet syrup tastes far better than store-bought. Keep it on hand in a squeeze bottle to produce a classic ice cream soda or the Stout Floats on page 20 (or drizzle it over ice cream).

Makes a scant I cup

½ cup (1.625 ounces) unsweetened cocoa powder, preferably natural

⅔ cup (4.625 ounces) sugar

Pinch of salt

⅔ cup water

1 teaspoon pure vanilla extract

Put the cocoa powder in a small bowl. Combine the sugar, salt, and water in a small saucepan, bring to a low boil, and boil for 2 minutes. Whisk enough of the hot syrup into the cocoa to form a smooth paste, then whisk in the remaining syrup. Stir in the vanilla. Let cool. The syrup can be stored in a squeeze bottle or a jar in the refrigerator for up to 3 weeks.

✳ GOOD TO KNOW

Use tiny pinches of salt to lift the flavor of the chocolate without making the sauce taste salty.

4 INDISPENSABLE CARAMEL SAUCES

Here are four grandly gooey sweet sauces to choose from, including the effortless Tropical Sugar Sauce that comes together in about six minutes and does not require that you caramelize the sugar. Brown sugar (versus white) makes the characteristic difference between caramel and butterscotch. And, in all cases, a little bit of salt accentuates flavors and keeps these old-fashioned favorites irresistibly up-to-date.

THE SIMPLEST CARAMEL SAUCE

This sauce is very clean—just sugar and cream with a bit of salt and vanilla, no corn syrup, or butter, or anything else.

Makes 1¼ cups

¾ cup heavy cream

½ cup water

1 cup (7 ounces) sugar

⅛ teaspoon salt, or to taste

1½ teaspoons pure vanilla extract

Set the cream near the stove.

Set a small white plate and a wooden skewer or a small knife near the stove. Pour the water into a 2-quart saucepan and set over medium heat. Add the sugar, pouring it in a thin stream into the center of the pan to form a low mound. Don't stir, but use your fingers to pat the sugar down until it is entirely moistened. Cook uncovered, without stirring, for a few minutes, until the sugar is dissolved. Continue to cook, without stirring, until the syrup begins to color slightly; swirl the pan gently if the caramel seems to be coloring unevenly. Use the skewer or the tip of the knife to drop a bead of syrup onto the plate from time to time (because the sauce always looks darker in the pan). Drops will look clear at first, then pale gold and amber. When a drop of caramel looks amber, immediately remove the pan from the heat. Holding the pan at arm's length, pour a generous gulp of cream into the pot. It will steam and bubble furiously. Add the remaining cream in 3 or 4 additions, one after the other. Stir over low heat to dissolve any caramel, then simmer for a minute or two. Off the heat, stir in the salt and vanilla. Serve warm or cool. The sauce keeps in a covered container in the refrigerator for at least several weeks.

BUTTERSCOTCH TOFFEE SAUCE

Butterscotch made with actual Scotch was the brilliant inspiration of Maya Klein, my frequent collaborator. This sauce has a delicious depth of flavor that may remind you of good English toffee candies. Don't miss this one.

Makes 1¼ cups

¾ cup heavy cream

½ cup water

2 tablespoons single-malt or blended Scotch

1 cup (7 ounces) firmly packed brown sugar

⅛ teaspoon salt, or to taste

1 teaspoon pure vanilla extract

Set the cream near the stove.

Pour the water and the Scotch into a 2-quart saucepan and set over medium heat. Sprinkle the brown sugar into the center of the pan to form a low mound. Don't stir, but use your fingers to pat the sugar down until it is entirely moistened. Cook uncovered, swirling the pan from time to time rather than stirring, until large bubbles form and break on the surface. Continue to cook, watching as the bubbles get smaller and thicker and slower all over the surface of the sauce.

Remove the pan from the heat and, holding it at arm's length, gradually pour in the cream. Stir over low heat to dissolve any thickened caramel, then simmer for a minute or two.

Off the heat, stir in the salt and vanilla. Serve warm or cool. The sauce keeps in a covered container in the refrigerator for at least several weeks.

TROPICAL SUGAR SAUCE

Muscovado and other raw sugars are so flavorful that all you need to do is simmer them with a little liquid and you've got a sensational sauce for coffee or vanilla ice cream, fresh pineapple, bananas, and more.

Makes 1¼ to 1½ cups

¾ cup (5.25 ounces) firmly packed raw sugar, such as light or dark muscovado, or grated piloncillo or palm sugar

1 cup heavy cream or ¾ cup water, coffee, coconut milk, or pineapple juice

⅛ teaspoon salt, or to taste

½ teaspoon rum (particularly good if using muscovado or piloncillo) or pure vanilla extract (particularly good if using palm sugar), optional

Whisk together the sugar, cream, and salt in a medium saucepan, bring to a simmer over low heat, and simmer for 5 minutes, stirring frequently. Add the rum or vanilla, if using. The sauce keeps in a covered container in the refrigerator for at least several weeks.

✳ VARIATIONS

Butterscotch Toffee Fondue

Give each guest a little cup of hot butterscotch sauce and set a platter of big crunchy cubes of toast, banana chunks, apple slices, etc., in the center of the table for all to help themselves.

Bananas or Pineapple Foster

Serve any caramel sauce over vanilla ice cream and sautéed (or raw) bananas or pineapple slices.

SPICE-DRAWER CINNAMON TOAST

Cinnamon toast—or any spiced-butter toast—is a marvelous crunchy dessert element, even if it's just to elevate a dish of ice cream or to accompany a cup of rich hot chocolate (dunk often). Looking for adventure? Open your spice drawer and sniff the contents of any jars you think might taste good on buttered toast. Substitute ground spices to taste for the cinnamon. Consider nutmeg, pumpkin pie spice, garam masala, cardamom, or cinnamon mixed with ginger, cloves, or cardamom.

Makes 8 to 12 toasts

INGREDIENTS

8 to 12 slices fresh or slightly stale baguette (sliced on the diagonal up to 1 inch thick and 6 inches long for maximum drama—or any size slices that you have on hand), or 4 to 6 slices regular bread, cut in half to make 8 or 12 pieces

¼ cup (1.75 ounces) firmly packed brown sugar (or raw sugar, such as muscovado or grated piloncillo or palm sugar) or plain white sugar

1 teaspoon ground cinnamon

2 tablespoons (1 ounce) unsalted butter, softened

Pinch or two of salt

EQUIPMENT

Baking sheet

DIRECTIONS

Preheat the broiler, with the rack 4 to 5 inches from the heating element, or use a toaster oven. Put the bread on the baking sheet. If your bread is fresh and you want a little extra crispness, toast the slices briefly before covering with the cinnamon mixture. Mix the sugar, cinnamon, butter, and salt together and spread on the bread. Broil until the edges of the bread are dark brown and the sugar is bubbly. Serve at once.

＊ **GOOD TO KNOW**
   6 More Things to Do with
   Spice-Drawer Cinnamon Toast

1] Serve with berries and cream or bananas and cream.

2] Serve with Creamy, Dreamy Rice Pudding (page 102).

3] Serve with chocolate pudding (see page 88).

4] Use instead of graham crackers to make s'mores.

5] Make dessert crostini: drizzle the toasts with melted dark chocolate and top with raspberries or banana slices.

6] Use as a raft for ice cream in bowls of double-strength Mexican hot chocolate (made with half the liquid called for in the package directions).

DESSERT CROUTONS

Here's a hip, playful dessert topper with super-crunchy texture and rich flavor from butter or fresh, bright olive oil. These are astonishing over a bowl of vanilla ice cream, naked or with chocolate or caramel sauce, or on the Honey Balsamic Sundaes (page 16). Note that the butter is brushed on the bread before toasting, but the oil is drizzled on the bread after it is toasted—this preserves all the flavors of the oil and produces a more exciting texture. These disappear quickly (because everyone snacks on them), hence the large recipe!

Makes about 4 cups

INGREDIENTS

½ round or wide loaf French bread, cut into ½-inch-thick slices

4 tablespoons (2 ounces) unsalted butter, melted, or ¼ cup flavorful but not too pungent extra virgin olive oil

Fleur de sel or other flaky salt (optional)

EQUIPMENT

Baking sheet

DIRECTIONS

Position a rack in the center of the oven and preheat the oven to 275°F.

Cut the bread slices into ½-inch cubes and heap on the baking sheet.

If using butter, drizzle it over the cubes, tossing gently to coat them, and then, if using salt, sprinkle with very tiny pinches (crushing large flakes slightly between your fingers) to taste. (If using oil, hold off on it and the salt.) Spread the cubes out on the baking sheet and toast for 25 to 35 minutes, tossing from time to time, until thoroughly dry and crunchy and golden.

If using oil, drizzle it over the cubes, tossing gently, and then, if using salt, add judiciously, as described above. Let the croutons cool.

※ **VARIATIONS**

Spicy Dessert Croutons

Make the croutons with butter. Before baking, toss with 2 tablespoons sugar mixed with ¼ teaspoon ground cinnamon.

Pecan Croutons

Mix the cooled croutons with 1 cup (3.5 ounces) toasted pecans, coarsely chopped.

COOKIE CRUNCH

Baked cookie crumbs mixed with butter and sugar make irresistibly crunchy and flavorful toppers for ice cream or anything creamy. Smash the cookies to crumbs in a plastic bag, or use the food processor, especially if you are pulverizing nuts too. You can taste and adjust the sweetness and spice in the crumb mixture before you bake, so it's easy to invent your own flavors. Here are four starter recipes, any of which can be used as a substitute crust for Chocolate Pudding Pie (page 139) or Milk Chocolate Pudding Pie with Salted Peanut Crust (page 137). Mix as directed and follow the instructions on page 136 for lining the pie pan and baking the crust.

GRAHAM CRACKER CRUNCH

Makes 1½ cups

1½ cups (5 ounces) graham cracker crumbs

¼ cup (1.75 ounces) sugar

6 tablespoons (3 ounces) unsalted butter, melted

Pinch or two of salt

Position a rack in the center of the oven and preheat the oven to 350°F. Line a baking sheet with parchment paper.

Mix all the ingredients together thoroughly. Dump the mixture onto the baking sheet and spread it about ¼ inch thick with a fork. Bake for 12 to 15 minutes, raking and spreading the mixture out again once or twice with the fork, until the mixture smells toasted and looks a shade more golden brown than it did before baking. Set the pan on a rack to cool. Break up the crunch. It can be stored in an airtight container for at least a week.

CHOCOLATE COOKIE CRUNCH

Makes 1½ cups

1½ cups (6.75 ounces) chocolate cookie crumbs (from about three-quarters of a 9-ounce package of chocolate wafers)

¼ cup (1.75 ounces) sugar

6 tablespoons (3 ounces) unsalted butter, melted

Mix and bake for 8 to 10 minutes, or until the mixture looks slightly drier and less buttery.

SPICY PECAN COOKIE CRUNCH

Makes 1⅓ cups

⅓ cup (1 ounce) pecan pieces, finely chopped or pulverized in a food processor

1 cup (3.4 ounces) graham cracker crumbs

3 tablespoons (1.3 ounces) sugar

¼ teaspoon salt

¼ teaspoon ground cinnamon

½ teaspoon ground ancho chile

4 tablespoons (2 ounces) unsalted butter, melted

Mix and bake as directed in the Graham Cracker Crunch recipe.

SALTED PEANUT COOKIE CRUNCH

Makes 1⅓ cups

⅓ cup (1.33 ounces) salted roasted peanuts, finely chopped or pulverized in a food processor

1 cup (3.4 ounces) graham cracker crumbs

3 tablespoons (1.3 ounces) sugar

4 tablespoons (2 ounces) unsalted butter, melted

Mix and bake as directed in the Graham Cracker Crunch recipe.

PRALINE

Praline is an element used in classical French pastry that deserves a bigger stage. It is simply caramelized sugar with nuts. Coarsely crushed, it makes a superlative crunchy garnish for cake or an ice cream sundae or a bowl of orange slices. Chopped fine or ground into a powder, it can be used to flavor whipped cream. It's versatile and simple to make. You can use any nut you fancy.

Makes about 2⅔ cups

INGREDIENTS

1 cup water

2 cups (14 ounces) sugar

2⅔ cups (9.3 ounces) coarsely chopped walnuts or pecans

EQUIPMENT

Baking sheet

DIRECTIONS

Line the baking sheet with foil or parchment paper and set near the stove, along with a skewer or a small knife and a small white plate. Pour the water into a 2- or 3-quart saucepan and set over medium heat. Add the sugar, pouring it in a thin stream into the center of the pan to form a low mound. Don't stir, but if necessary, use your fingers to pat the sugar down until it is entirely moistened. Cover the pan and cook, without stirring, for a few minutes until the sugar is dissolved. Uncover the pan and cook, without stirring, until the syrup begins to color slightly. Swirl the pan gently if the caramel seems to be coloring unevenly.

Use the skewer or the tip of the knife to drop a bead of syrup onto the plate from time to time. When a drop of caramel looks pale amber, add the nuts and turn them gently with a silicone spatula or a wooden spoon just until completely coated. (Brisk stirring will cause the caramel to crystallize.) Continue to cook, pushing the nuts around gently if the caramel is coloring

⁕ GOOD TO KNOW

A silicone spatula makes it easy to scrape the mixture from the pan—and it's easy to clean.

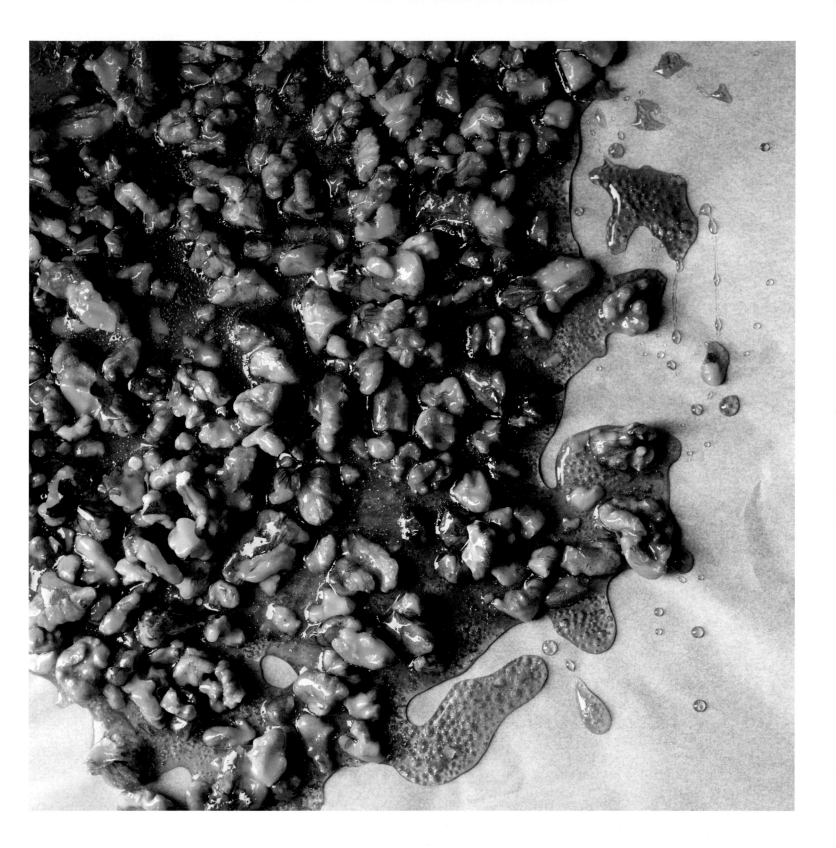

unevenly, until a drop of caramel looks deep amber on the plate. Immediately scrape the mixture onto the lined baking sheet and spread it out as well as you can.

When it is cool enough to handle but still quite warm, break the praline into pieces and transfer it (yes, still warm) to a zip-lock bag or an airtight container, to prevent it from getting sticky. Keep airtight until needed.

When ready to use, break the praline into smaller pieces and chop or pulse in a food processor.

EASY ICE CREAMS AND SHERBETS WITHOUT AN ICE CREAM MACHINE

Many cooks avoid making ice cream because they don't have an ice cream machine, or they hate hauling it from the basement or cupboard, or they are a little scared of making the traditional custard base. But if you own a food processor or a blender, you can make terrific ice creams very easily. And some of the best do not involve any sort of custard base. Some of the following recipes start out with mixtures that are made like fruit smoothies; others begin with a few ingredients simply stirred together. It's a two-and-a-half-step process: mix the ingredients (usually no cooking) and freeze in a shallow container; break up and process the chunks in a food processor or blender until creamy; and refreeze. Then just serve! Among the bonuses to making your own ice cream: no preservatives or artificial flavors or high-fructose corn syrup; control over sweetness and richness (I find commercial ice creams too sweet and too rich most of the time); and lots of room for experimentation, with a high success rate.

I chose the recipes here because they are unusual flavors that you can't buy, or they are better than what you can buy, or they are just so simple and so good that I couldn't help myself.

Many of these ice creams are less rich than the usual ice creams that you buy, because the most innovative and best new ice creams that I have tasted are more focused on flavor than on richness. Some of my recipes call for milk, even low-fat milk, rather than cream, and no eggs at all. Lighter ice creams, sherbets, and sorbets allow flavors to pop; they are extra refreshing. Expect great big flavors and interesting new combinations.

CREATE YOUR OWN ICE CREAMS AND SHERBETS

If you want to experiment, start with these recipes and try your own variations. Note that too much sugar will prevent the mixture from freezing properly, as will too much alcohol. Fruit with lots of fiber (like bananas, mangoes, and persimmons) will produce creamier results than fruits with less fiber. Water, fruit juice, or low-fat milk will make fruit flavors brighter and tangy flavors more tangy, while richer milk or cream makes flavors milder and textures creamier and more luxurious.

PEACHES 'N' SOUR CREAM ICE CREAM

Homemade peach ice cream is fresher and more peachy than any you can buy. The secret here is using cream or sour cream instead of a traditional custard for the base. And it's quicker too.

Makes 1 pint

INGREDIENTS

1 to 2 medium to large peaches

1 tablespoon fresh lemon juice

½ cup (3.5 ounces) sugar

1 cup sour cream

EQUIPMENT

Food processor or blender

DIRECTIONS

Peel the peaches and remove the pits. Cut enough fruit into 1-inch chunks to make 1 very firmly packed cup. (Nibble any leftover fruit or reserve it for another use.) Puree the peaches with the lemon juice in the food processor or blender until fairly smooth (the mixture will get even smoother in the second processing). Add the sugar and sour cream and pulse just to mix. Scrape the mixture into a shallow pan, cover, and freeze.

Break the frozen mixture into small chunks with a fork and process in the food processor or blender until blended and smooth. If some of the frozen chunks are stubborn, don't be afraid to continue processing: extra processing only makes smoother, creamier ice cream. Serve immediately as a slushy spoon drink, or scrape into a container and refreeze until firm enough to scoop, at least 3 hours.

If the ice cream freezes solid, let it soften in the fridge for 15 minutes or longer, or carefully soften it in the microwave on the defrost setting, a few seconds at a time. For the best flavor and texture, serve within 2 to 3 days.

✱ VARIATION

Peaches 'n' Sweet Cream Ice Cream

Increase the lemon juice to 2 tablespoons and substitute heavy cream for the sour cream.

PINEAPPLE ICE CREAM

Starting with a can of frozen pineapple juice concentrate may seem like cheating, but this creamy and very pineappley ice cream is so good that I prefer to think of it as a rabbit from a hat: an easy, impressive dessert made in the food processor. Serve it with nothing at all, or with coconut cookies or strawberries.

Makes a scant 1 quart

INGREDIENTS

One 12-ounce can frozen pineapple juice concentrate

2 cups heavy cream

½ cup water

½ cup (3.5 ounces) sugar

EQUIPMENT

Food processor or blender

DIRECTIONS

Combine all the ingredients in a medium bowl and stir until the sugar is dissolved. Let stand for 2 to 3 minutes, then stir again to be sure that the sugar is completely dissolved. Scrape the mixture into a shallow pan, cover, and freeze.

Break the frozen mixture into small chunks with a fork and process in the food processor or blender until blended and smooth. If some of the frozen chunks are stubborn, don't be afraid to continue processing: extra processing only makes smoother, creamier ice cream. Serve immediately as a slushy spoon drink, or scrape into a container and refreeze until firm enough to scoop, at least 3 hours.

If the ice cream freezes solid, let it soften in the fridge for 15 minutes or longer, or carefully soften it in the microwave on the defrost setting, a few seconds at a time. For the best flavor and texture, serve within 2 to 3 days.

✳ VARIATIONS

Mini Banana Split

Serve with a scoop of vanilla ice cream, sliced bananas, toasted macadamia or other nuts, and chocolate sauce.

Fresh Lychee Sundae

Serve in a shallow bowl with a moat of coconut milk and fresh lychees.

Pineapple Mango Sherbet

Substitute 12 ounces plain low-fat yogurt for the heavy cream. Puree 1 heaping cup fresh ripe or frozen mango chunks in a food processor and blend with the other ingredients before freezing the first time.

Pineapple Banana Sherbet

Substitute 12 ounces plain low-fat yogurt for the heavy cream. Reduce the sugar to ¼ cup. Puree 1 heaping cup banana chunks in a food processor and blend with the other ingredients before freezing the first time.

COCONUT LIME SHERBET

It's easy to keep the ingredients for this spectacular sherbet—tangy, tropical, and totally refreshing—on hand. Regular coconut milk makes a creamier sherbet, but low-fat wins for brighter flavor and a more refreshing result. You choose.

Makes 3⅓ cups

INGREDIENTS

2⅔ cups low-fat (also called "light") or regular unsweetened coconut milk

1 cup (7 ounces) sugar

1½ teaspoons grated regular lime or Key lime zest

½ cup fresh lime juice (from 6 to 7 regular limes or 8 to 10 Key limes)

EQUIPMENT

Food processor or blender

DIRECTIONS

Combine all of the ingredients in a medium bowl and stir until the sugar is dissolved. Let stand for 2 to 3 minutes, then stir again to be sure that the sugar is completely dissolved.

Pour the mixture into a shallow pan, cover, and freeze until hard, 3 to 4 hours.

Break the frozen mixture into chunks with a fork, and process in the food processor or blender until the mixture is smooth and the color has lightened. If some of the frozen chunks are stubborn, don't be afraid to continue processing: extra processing only makes smoother, creamier sherbet. Serve immediately as a slushy spoon drink, or transfer to an airtight container and refreeze until hard enough to scoop, 3 to 4 hours.

If the sherbet freezes too hard, let it soften in the fridge for 15 minutes or longer, or carefully soften it in the microwave on the defrost setting, a few seconds at a time. For the best flavor and texture, serve within 2 to 3 days.

✳ **GOOD TO KNOW**

Unsweetened coconut milk traditionally comes in cans. However, you can substitute the very lightly sweetened coconut milk (such as Silk Pure Coconut) that comes in cartons in the refrigerated section of the supermarket near the milk.

LEMON MINT SHERBET

Fresh and sparkling on the palate. Try the herbal variation, or omit the mint to make plain lemon sherbet.

Makes 3⅓ cups

INGREDIENTS

A very large handful of fresh mint leaves

1 cup (7 ounces) sugar

½ cup fresh lemon juice (from about 3 medium lemons; grate the zest before juicing the lemons)

2⅔ cups 1% or whole milk

1½ teaspoons grated lemon zest (preferably organic or unsprayed)

EQUIPMENT

Strainer

Food processor or blender

DIRECTIONS

Reserve a few mint leaves for garnish. Stir the sugar, lemon juice, and remaining mint leaves together in a medium bowl. Let stand for 1 hour.

Stir the milk into the lemon juice mixture, then strain the mixture through the sieve into a bowl, pressing lightly on the mint leaves; discard the mint. Add the lemon zest. The mixture will thicken slightly and may look curdled—this is okay. Pour the mixture into a shallow pan, cover, and freeze until hard, 3 to 4 hours.

Break the frozen mixture into chunks with a fork, and process in the food processor or blender until the mixture is smooth and the color has lightened. If some of the frozen chunks are stubborn, don't be afraid to continue processing: extra processing only makes smoother, creamier sherbet.

Continued

Continued

✳ VARIATIONS

Lemon Basil Sherbet

Substitute a large handful of fresh basil leaves for the mint.

Plain Lemon Sherbet

Omit the mint leaves. Let the lemon juice mixture stand for only 3 minutes, then stir to be sure the sugar is dissolved. Skip the straining step.

Lemon Rose Sherbet

Omit the mint leaves. Let the lemon juice mixture stand for only 3 minutes, then stir to be sure the sugar is dissolved. Skip the straining step. Add 1 to 2 teaspoons rose water, to taste, with the lemon zest. After processing the frozen mixture, taste it and correct the flavor with additional drops of rose water, if necessary.

Serve immediately as a slushy spoon drink, garnished with the reserved mint leaves, or transfer to an airtight container and refreeze until hard enough to scoop, 3 to 4 hours.

If the sherbet freezes too hard, let it soften in the fridge for 15 minutes or longer, or carefully soften it in the microwave on the defrost setting, a few seconds at a time. For the best flavor and texture, serve within 2 to 3 days.

✳ NANCY Z'S MARGARITA ICE

My friend Nancy Zaslavski is the author of several Mexican cookbooks. Here's a refreshing and spirited dessert that's perfect for outdoor entertaining: Put 6 purchased lime ice pops in a bowl and sprinkle them with ¼ cup 100% agave tequila and the juice of a fresh lime. Pass out napkins and then pass the bowl of pops followed by a shallow dish of coarse or flaky sea salt. Each guest takes a pop and dips it into— or sprinkles it with—a little bit of salt. The juices left in the bottom of the bowl are the cook's treat.

COFFEE GRANITA

Granita is sophisticated shaved ice: super-flavorful, not too sweet little shards of ice, usually made with lemon juice or espresso, but equally delicious made with wine or even beer or stout (see the variations). Granita is ultrarefreshing on a hot day, plain or with whipped cream on top. Less obviously, it is extremely good and a bit dressy served as a topping over vanilla ice cream. The yin-yang of creamy with icy, mellow with intense, is quietly spectacular.

Makes about 3 cups

INGREDIENTS

2 cups very strong freshly brewed coffee

4 to 6 tablespoons (1.75 to 2.625 ounces) sugar

DIRECTIONS

Mix the coffee with the sugar to taste: the mixture should be strong and a bit sweeter than you ultimately want it to be, because freezing mutes sweetness. Stir to dissolve the sugar. Pour the mixture into a shallow pan and put it in the freezer until partially frozen, 1½ to 2 hours.

Use a fork to scrape and break the mixture into shards and crystals. Return the pan to the freezer to freeze completely.

When it is frozen, scrape and toss the mixture one more time with the fork. Keep frozen until ready to serve.

✳ VARIATIONS

Lemon Granita

Substitute 1 cup fresh lemon juice (from 6 to 7 lemons; with pulp is okay) for the coffee and increase the sugar to 6 or 7 tablespoons. Dissolve the sugar in 1 cup hot water before adding the lemon juice.

Wine or Beer Granita

Substitute 1 cup dry red or white wine or rosé (or a combination of any leftover, still-drinkable wine) or a light ale or pilsner or wheat beer (but nothing as bitter as India pale ale) for the coffee. Use 3 tablespoons sugar and dissolve it in 6 tablespoons hot water before adding the wine or beer. (Makes about 2 cups.)

THAI TEA ICE WITH SWEET MILK

What Thai food fan doesn't love Thai iced tea? And shouldn't everyone know about it? Here, it is deconstructed and made into an exotic and refreshing dessert: strong, spicy tea granita—a tad bitter—with super-rich sweet milk. Really simple; really good.

Serves 6

INGREDIENTS

2¼ cups water

½ cup Thai tea leaves (see Resources, page 277)

2 tablespoons sugar

½ cup sweetened condensed milk

½ cup whole milk

EQUIPMENT

Basket-type (round) coffee filter or a sieve lined with a double layer of paper towels

DIRECTIONS

Bring the water to a boil in a medium saucepan. Remove from the heat, stir in the tea leaves, cover, and let steep for 7 minutes.

Pour the tea through the coffee filter or the lined sieve into a bowl; discard the tea leaves. Stir the sugar into the tea until dissolved. Pour the tea into a shallow pan and put it in the freezer until almost completely frozen, 1½ to 2 hours.

Use a fork to scrape and break the mixture into shards and crystals. Return the pan to the freezer to freeze completely.

Meanwhile, mix the condensed milk with the whole milk; chill in the refrigerator.

When the granita is frozen, scrape and toss it one more time with the fork. Keep frozen until serving. To serve, divide the milk mixture among six glasses and top with the tea granita.

* **VARIATION**

Vietnamese Coffee Ice with Sweet Milk

Substitute ½ cup finely ground French-roast coffee beans (decaf is fine) for the tea leaves and steep for 5 minutes instead of 7.

STARTING WITH FRUIT

No dessert evokes time and place like a fruit dessert. From the sauté pan hot and fast, or gently poached, macerated, or baked, fruit is seasonal. It's light, it's sweet, it's simple yet beguiling on the palate. Baked with sugar, fruit makes its own jewel-toned sauce. It's juicy or slurpy, tart and sweet, and it's the best way to finish a rich meal. Fruit is versatile: it loves a crispy or crusty or tender cakey topping or accompaniment, and it invites spices. It's fragrant when hot, and flavorful when cool. It goes with cake, it goes with ice cream, and it stands alone. Shop at the farmers' market, produce stand, supermarket, or corner grocery, but let the fruit beckon, and shop like a chef, with more than one recipe in mind: opt for the plum crisp when plums look better than peaches, and don't even think of dipping strawberries in chocolate if the berries are not ripe. Get friendly with your produce guy or gal, and ask for tastes before buying. Eschew the frugal wisdom of using overripe or mushy fruit for cooking: if it doesn't taste good, don't waste your time and ingredients.

THINGS TO DO WITH RIPE STRAWBERRIES

Top with

- Whipped cream. If the berries are really ripe and sweet, don't even sweeten the cream; just add a little vanilla (or nothing at all). You will be surprised at how the strawberry flavor will pop.

- Coffee Whipped Cream (page 131), Fresh Mint Whipped Cream (page 132), Halvah Whipped Cream (page 132), Praline Whipped Cream (page 132), White Chocolate Whipped Cream (page 133), or Rose Whipped Cream (page 131).

- Crumbled halvah or chopped pistachios and Rose Whipped Cream (page 131) or whipped cream.

- Crushed amaretti, store-bought or homemade (page 240), or crushed Praline (page 32) and whipped cream.

Serve

- Sliced and sugared to taste, with Buttermilk Panna Cotta (page 106).

- Sliced, with Honey Balsamic Sundaes (page 16).

- Sliced, over ice cream with Chocolate Sauce "to Taste" (page 23) or Cocoa Fudge Sauce (page 23).

- Sliced, with Crunchy Almond Butter Meringue (page 164), Coconut Meringue (page 166), or Classic Pavlova (page 161).

- Sliced and sugared to taste, with Sour Cream and Brown Sugar Tart (page 147).

Dip in

- Chocolate, of course (see page 264).

Toss whole, or halved if large, with

- Balsamic vinegar and fresh mint leaves (or a grinding of black pepper) and sugar to taste. Serve with ricotta, fromage blanc, or a mild, creamy goat cheese.

- Liqueurs, spirits, or fortified wine.

Improvise

- Serve with bowls of sour cream (or labneh or yogurt) and dark brown or muscovado sugar. Guests dip individual berries in cream, then in sugar.

- Serve sliced or quartered over vanilla ice cream with a shot of single-malt Scotch poured over.

- Drain regular or Greek yogurt, stir in sugar and brandy (or orange zest and juice) to taste, and top with sliced strawberries and toasted almonds.

- Garnish a bowl of ricotta or Greek yogurt with sliced strawberries, drizzle with honey, and sprinkle with chopped almonds or pistachios.

- Pour red wine over whole strawberries or sliced stone fruit, adding about 2 tablespoons of sugar per cup of wine and a squeeze of lemon juice. Let macerate at room temperature for up to an hour, then chill for no more than another hour, to keep the fruit firm and fresh tasting. Serve the fruit with a little of its liquid. (Photograph on page 46.) You can simmer any leftover liquid until it is thickened and syrupy and use it to sauce fruit or ice cream.

SAUTÉED FIGS

Serve this quick-fire dish with blue cheese and shortbread cookies, or with goat cheese or aged cheddar. Greek yogurt or vanilla ice cream? Always good. With the latter, consider passing a cruet of extra virgin olive oil for drizzling.

Serves 8

INGREDIENTS

4 tablespoons (2 ounces) unsalted butter

½ cup (3.5 ounces) sugar

⅛ teaspoon salt

1 pound ripe figs, stemmed and halved (4 cups)

2 tablespoons fresh lemon juice

½ teaspoon ground cinnamon

DIRECTIONS

Combine the butter, sugar, and salt in a large skillet and cook over high heat until the butter melts and starts to color. Turn the heat down to medium, add the figs and lemon juice all at once, and cook, stirring once or twice, until the fruit is slightly softened, 1 to 3 minutes.

Remove from the heat and sprinkle with the cinnamon. Serve hot or warm. The figs keep in the refrigerator for several days.

✳ **GOOD TO KNOW**

Squishy, even oozy, figs are riper and tastier than firm figs.

✳ **VARIATIONS**

Sautéed Peaches

Serve with toasted walnuts or pecans over ice cream or topped with whipped cream.

Substitute 1½- to 2-inch chunks of peaches (with their skin) for the figs, brown sugar for the white, and nutmeg for the cinnamon.

Sautéed or Grilled Pineapple with Coffee Ice Cream
(photograph on page 2)

Substitute 1½- to 2-inch chunks of fresh pineapple for the figs. Or cut the pineapple into ½-inch slices, brush with a little melted butter, and grill on a grill or in a hot grill pan until browned. Serve with coffee ice cream and, especially if grilled, any of the Caramel Sauces on pages 25–26 or Chocolate Sauce "to Taste," page 23.

APPLES IN CARDAMOM LIME SYRUP

Apple compote may sound boring, but this one is spectacular—far more than the sum of its parts. Serve it alone, or with nut or coconut cookies. Or add a dollop of Greek yogurt or crème fraîche or a scoop of coconut ice cream. Both the apple and the pear variations are good partners for Fresh Ginger Gingerbread (page 213). The leftover syrup makes a terrific cocktail or flavored soda; see the variation.

Serves 4 to 6

INGREDIENTS

16 cardamom pods

1⅓ cups water

⅔ cup fresh lime juice (from 9 to 10 limes)

1¾ cups (12.25 ounces) sugar

3 medium-large firm, flavorful apples (such as Red Delicious, Granny Smith, pippins, Pink Lady, Sierra Beauty, or Braeburn), with skins left on, cut into 8 or 10 wedges

DIRECTIONS

Gently smash the cardamom pods with a heavy object.

Combine the water, lime juice, cardamom, and sugar in a medium nonreactive saucepan and bring to a boil over high heat, then turn the heat down to medium and simmer for 5 minutes.

Add the apples to the simmering syrup and set a salad plate or a saucer (slightly smaller in diameter than the pan) on the apples to keep them submerged. Simmer for 8 to 10 minutes, until just tender when pierced with a toothpick.

Remove from the heat and let the apples cool without removing the saucer for about an hour, then chill them in the syrup. The apples keep in the refrigerator for at least a week. They get better with time. Serve chilled.

✳ VARIATIONS

Apple Cardamom Soda or Sparkling Cocktail

For the soda, use 1 part leftover cardamom lime syrup to 4 parts sparkling water; for the cocktail, use 1 part syrup to 1 part vodka or gin and 3 parts sparkling water. Garnish with a mint sprig.

Pears in Ginger Lemon Syrup

Substitute six ⅛-inch-thick slices fresh ginger for the cardamom and substitute lemon juice for the lime. Substitute 4 to 5 medium Bartlett or Comice pears, quartered and cored, for the apples, and simmer for 3 to 5 minutes. Cool and chill as for apples.

Pears in Fennel Lemon Syrup

Substitute ½ teaspoon fennel seeds for the ginger.

FB'S VANILLA PEAR AND APPLE COMPOTE

London artist and jewelry designer Frances Bendixson has been a great friend and creative inspiration to me since I was twenty. Our last dinner together commenced with a drink at her kitchen table while we prepared the pears and apples for this dessert. We enjoyed it warm with a little yogurt, but you can pour some heavy cream over it, or plop a dollop of whipped cream or ice cream on it. I like the compote even better chilled; it improves with time (just as we have!).

Makes 6 cups

INGREDIENTS

4 to 5 firm, ripe pears (such as Comice, Bartlett, or Bosc, or a combination)

4 to 5 firm, flavorful apples (such as Red Delicious, Granny Smith, pippins, Pink Lady, Sierra Beauty, or Braeburn, or a combination)

¼ cup (1.75 ounces) sugar, or more to taste

1 vanilla bean, split

⅓ cup water

DIRECTIONS

Peel, quarter, and core the fruit and cut each quarter into 2 or 3 chunks. Put in a large saucepan with the sugar, vanilla bean, and water, cover, and cook over medium-low heat, stirring from time to time, until the fruit is tender and the mixture resembles a very chunky sauce, 30 to 45 minutes. Add a little water if the pot gets dry. Toward the end of cooking, taste and correct the sweetness and uncover the pot if there is too much liquid. Serve warm or chilled. Store the compote in the refrigerator with the vanilla bean, which will continue to impart flavor; it keeps for at least a week.

✱ TIP

Feeling frugal? You can use the whole vanilla bean without splitting it. After the compote is consumed (however long that takes) retrieve, rinse, and dry the bean and put it away to use another day.

THE VIRTUES OF VANILLA

Pure vanilla extract tastes better than imitation extract. I use Tahitian, Mexican, or Bourbon, depending on the flavor I'm looking for. Tahitian has a floral aroma, like exotic tropical flowers, with flavor notes of cherry, licorice, and raisins. Mexican vanilla has aromas of rum and caramel and very ripe fruit. Bourbon vanilla (also called Madagascar), the type most familiar to North Americans, is most difficult to describe because it smells and tastes like . . . well, vanilla.

Whole vanilla beans add exquisite flavor when steeped in liquid, either whole or split open with the tip of a paring knife and the seeds scraped into the liquid. I use them in custards and sauces and poaching liquids.

A LIFELONG SUPPLY OF VANILLA SUGAR

Vanilla beans are expensive—here's how to get the most from your investment. If beans are steeped whole, they can be rinsed and reused several times. When they seem to have lost their flavor, split them to expose the seeds, which will still be extremely flavorful, and use them again, scraping the seeds into the liquid. Finally, rather than discard the split pod pieces, rinse and dry them and stick them into a large container of sugar; replace the sugar you use with fresh sugar and continue to add your spent pods.

WHAT TO DO WITH VANILLA SUGAR?

Use it in place of plain sugar to sweeten your tea, coffee, or hot cocoa. Toss it with berries. Roll balls of cookie dough in it, or sprinkle it over sugar cookies before baking. Use it to replace the sugar in custards or sauces, flans or bread pudding, meringues or pavlovas, or poached pears or baked apples.

FRESH CHERRIES 3 WAYS

It's hard to stop eating fresh cherries in their season, but eventually you may be tempted to cook a few. Depending on your mood and inclination, you can serve any of these compotes hot, warm, or cold, perhaps in a little dish with an amaretti cookie or two. Or spoon around scoops of vanilla ice cream or over Sour Cream Soufflés (page 123). Or serve with a little fromage blanc topped with toasted almonds and cracked black pepper.

CHERRIES WITH BALSAMIC VINEGAR

Balsamic vinegar adds a little zing to quickly cooked cherries.

Serves 4 as a compote, 6 to 8 as an accompaniment

1 pound (3 cups) ripe cherries

2 tablespoons sugar

1 tablespoon balsamic vinegar

½ teaspoon grated lemon zest

1 tablespoon fresh lemon juice

Pinch of salt

Pit and halve the cherries (if you don't have a cherry pitter, halve them, then pit). Toss them in a bowl with the sugar, balsamic vinegar, lemon zest and juice, and salt. Let stand for 5 minutes or so to dissolve the sugar.

Heat a wide nonreactive skillet over medium-high heat until it is hot enough that a cherry sizzles when you toss it in. Add the cherries and their juices and cook, scraping the bottom of the pan frequently to prevent the juices from burning, just long enough to reduce the juices to a thick, sticky glaze; this should take only a couple of minutes. Scrape the glazed cherries into a bowl and refrigerate. The compote keeps in the refrigerator for at least a week.

CHERRIES WITH KIRSCH

This one is especially good with Almond Cake (page 202) or Amaretti (page 240) made with walnuts.

Serves 4 as a compote, 6 to 8 as an accompaniment

1 pound (3 cups) ripe cherries

3 tablespoons kirsch

1 tablespoon sugar

1 teaspoon fresh lemon juice

Pinch of salt

Pit and halve the cherries (if you don't have a cherry pitter, halve them, then pit). Toss them in a bowl with the kirsch, sugar, lemon juice, and salt. Let stand for 5 minutes or so to dissolve the sugar.

Heat a wide nonreactive skillet over medium-high heat until it is hot enough that a cherry sizzles when you toss it in. Add the cherries and their juices and cook, scraping the bottom of the pan frequently to prevent the juices from burning, just long enough to reduce the juices to a thick, sticky glaze; this should take only a couple of minutes. Scrape the glazed cherries into a bowl and refrigerate. The compote keeps in the refrigerator for at least a week.

CHERRIES WITH VANILLA BEAN

These get better and better as they sit in the fridge, drawing flavor from the vanilla bean.

Serves 4 as a compote, 6 to 8 as an accompaniment

1 pound (3 cups) ripe cherries

3 tablespoons vodka

2 tablespoons sugar

½ vanilla bean

Pinch of salt

Fresh lemon juice, to taste

Split the piece of vanilla bean in half horizontally.

Pit and halve the cherries (if you don't have a cherry pitter, halve them, then pit). Toss them in a bowl with the vodka, sugar, vanilla bean pieces, and salt. Let stand for 5 minutes or so to dissolve the sugar.

Heat a wide nonreactive skillet over medium-high heat until it is hot enough that a cherry sizzles when you toss it in. Add the cherries and their juices and cook, scraping the bottom of the pan frequently to prevent the juices from burning, just long enough to reduce the juices to a thick, sticky glaze; this should take only a couple of minutes. Scrape the glazed cherries into a bowl and taste, adding a few drops of lemon juice if necessary to brighten the flavor. Leave the vanilla bean pieces in the mixture and refrigerate. The compote keeps in the refrigerator for at least a week.

CHEATING WITH FROZEN CHERRIES

When you just gotta have 'em and they just aren't in season. Here's how to make any of the preceding recipes using frozen cherries:

Thaw a 12-ounce bag of whole frozen cherries in a strainer set over a bowl, leaving them long enough to release at least 3 tablespoons of juice. Pour the juice into a cup and set aside. Dump the cherries into the bowl with the flavor ingredients called for in the recipe and proceed as directed, cooking on high heat to evaporate the juices quickly so that the cherries cook as briefly as possible. After scraping the glazed cherries back into the bowl, add the reserved cherry juice to the skillet and simmer for a minute or two until the juice is reduced and thickened; the bubbles will be large and foamy. Scrape the syrup into the bowl with the cherries. Taste and correct the flavor with drops or pinches of extra flavoring from the recipe: balsamic vinegar, lemon juice and/or zest, sugar, etc.

✳ TIP

Pitting cherries is splashy work—don't wear your best duds.

✳ GOOD TO KNOW

For toothsome rather than mushy cherries, a skillet that seems too large is better than a smaller one. If the cherries are crowded in the pan (or the heat is too low) they end up simmered (instead of sautéed) for too long in too much juice.

HONEY-CARAMELIZED FIGS

Here's a sweet, gooey treatment for figs, caramelized in honey, with a little pan sauce made by dissolving the caramelized honey in wine or fruit juice. Serve with fresh goat cheese, or a spoonful of mascarpone, or a bowl of vanilla ice cream, or just on its own.

INGREDIENTS

Honey

Salt

2 to 4 ripe figs per person, stemmed and halved

Walnut halves or pieces (optional)

Sherry (on the sweet side, or even quite sweet), port, or sweet Madeira

Squeeze of fresh lemon or orange juice (optional)

Pepper in a pepper grinder (optional)

DIRECTIONS

Choose a skillet large enough to hold the figs without crowding. Heat the empty skillet over fairly high heat, adding enough honey to melt and coat the pan. Sprinkle with a few tiny pinches of salt. As soon as the honey is hot and bubbly, arrange the figs cut side down in the pan and let the honey bubble and start to caramelize, shaking the pan to slide the figs around; watch carefully, adjusting the heat as necessary to prevent the honey from burning. When the cut side of a fig looks a little brown and caramelized, add the walnuts, if desired. Flip the figs (and walnuts) over and quickly coat them with glaze, then scrape onto a serving plate.

Return the pan to the heat and add enough sherry, port, or Madeira to dissolve the caramel left in the pan and form a syrupy sauce—let it bubble, but don't let it reduce down to thick caramel again, or it will harden like candy on the figs; add more liquid as necessary and adjust the flavor with a squeeze of citrus if necessary. Scrape the sauce over the figs. Serve hot or cool with a grind of fresh pepper, if desired.

BAKED FIGS WITH HONEY
AND BALSAMIC VINEGAR

These are divine served with fresh ricotta or fromage blanc, Greek yogurt, or crème fraîche or mascarpone.

Serves 6

INGREDIENTS

1 pound ripe figs, stemmed, left whole or halved

2 tablespoons honey, or to taste

1 tablespoon balsamic vinegar, or to taste

Pinch of salt

EQUIPMENT

1½- to 2-quart baking dish, about 2 inches deep

DIRECTIONS

Position a rack in the lower third of the oven and preheat the oven to 375°F.

Put the figs in the baking dish and drizzle with the honey and vinegar. Sprinkle with the salt. Cover the dish tightly with foil and bake for 1 hour if using whole figs or 30 to 40 minutes if they are halved, or until the figs are very tender and the juices are thickened and syrupy (they will thicken further on cooling). If the juices are still thin and copious toward the end of baking, uncover the dish for the last 10 to 15 minutes, checking frequently. Alternatively, if the syrup gets too thick before the figs are soft, add a little water. Toward the end of baking, taste the syrup and adjust to your taste with honey or vinegar if needed.

Serve the figs warm, hot, cool, or cold. They keep in a covered container in the refrigerator for at least a week; they can be reheated in the microwave.

✳ VARIATION

Baked Figs with Honey and Lemon

Omit the balsamic vinegar. Grate the zest from half a lemon. Then squeeze the juice from the whole lemon. Drizzle the figs with the honey and lemon juice, scatter the zest over them, and bake as directed.

IN PRAISE OF CRISPS AND COBBLERS

There is nothing fiddly or fussy about these soul-satisfying, juicy, tart, and sweet desserts with their cakey or crunchy or delicately crispy toppings. Most start with fruit and sugar mixed right in the baking dish. Depending on the type of fruit and the type of topping, some are baked until the fruit is hot and bubbly before the topping is added (to avoid a raw or soggy topping), while others go into the oven completely assembled. They are simple either way.

Use the lesser or greater sugar measure depending on the sweetness or tartness of your fruit and your own taste. In general, though, you can't go wrong by using an amount in the middle of the range given. Or start with the minimum and taste the sugared fruit before adding more. Keep in mind that the fruit will taste less sweet after it's cooked. (If the recipe calls for baking the fruit before adding the topping, you can taste a little of the hot fruit and make a sugar adjustment then if necessary.) I prefer to err on the tart side, because a scoop of ice cream or sweetened whipped cream always balances a tart dessert. Don't worry, you'll see.

You can play with these recipes by exchanging toppings from one cobbler or crisp to the next, or using a new or different fruit or mixing stone fruit with berries, or adding chopped dried fruits, grated citrus zest or favorite spices, even sprigs of fresh herbs, to the fruit.

APPLE CRISP

I leave the skins on the apples for the flavor and body they contribute. If you include some red apples in the mix, you will love the rosy-colored filling. If you are in a hurry, skip the dried apricots and orange zest and juice—as my daughter often does. The crisp is terrific warm or at room temperature, but it is especially flavorful cold, even after two or three or four days in the fridge (if it lasts that long!). Whipped cream is always nice, but it's not essential.

Serves 6 to 8

INGREDIENTS

FOR THE TOPPING

½ cup (2.25 ounces) unbleached all-purpose flour

½ cup (1.65 ounces) rolled oats

1 scant cup (3 ounces) coarsely chopped walnuts

½ cup (3.5 ounces) sugar

5 tablespoons (2.5 ounces) unsalted butter, melted

⅛ teaspoon salt

FOR THE FILLING

Grated zest and juice of 1 orange

½ cup (2.5 ounces) dried apricots, coarsely chopped

¼ to ½ cup sugar (1.75 to 3.5 ounces), depending on the tartness of the apples

1 teaspoon ground cinnamon

6 medium apples

EQUIPMENT

2-quart baking dish, about 2 inches deep

* GOOD TO KNOW

Apples for Baking

Use crisp, flavorful apples with a decent balance of sweetness and acidity, such as pippins, Granny Smiths, Sierra Beauties, and/or new-crop Jonathans, or a mixture.

DIRECTIONS

Position a rack in the lower third of the oven and preheat the oven to 350°F. Liberally butter the baking dish.

TO MAKE THE TOPPING Combine all the ingredients in a bowl and mix well. Set aside.

TO MAKE THE FILLING Combine the orange zest, juice, and chopped apricots in a small bowl. Let the apricots soften while you prepare the apples.

Mix the sugar and cinnamon in a large bowl. Quarter and core the apples. Cut each quarter into 3 or 4 chunks. Toss the apples with the cinnamon sugar. Stir in the apricots and juice.

Scrape the mixture into the buttered baking dish and spread it evenly. Distribute the crumbly topping evenly over the apples. Bake for 1¼ to 1½ hours, until the crisp is browned on top and the juices are bubbling and thickened. (If your apples were a little dry, you may not see any juices toward the end of the baking time; if so, the browned topping is your cue to doneness.) Serve warm or cold.

PEACH CRISP

Here, crunchy sweet oats and walnuts with brown sugar team up with ripe, juicy peaches. If you plan to serve the crisp with vanilla ice cream, keep the sugar on the low side so the fruit contrasts nicely with its sweet, creamy partner.

Serves 6

INGREDIENTS

FOR THE FILLING

2½ pounds peaches, halved, pitted, and cut into 1½-inch chunks (6 cups)

3 tablespoons unbleached all-purpose flour

⅓ to ⅔ cup (2.33 to 4.625 ounces) sugar, depending on the sweetness of the peaches

¾ teaspoon ground cinnamon

FOR THE TOPPING

½ cup (2.25 ounces) unbleached all-purpose flour

½ cup (1.65 ounces) rolled oats

1 cup (3.5 ounces) walnuts, coarsely chopped

½ cup (3.5 ounces) firmly packed brown sugar

4 tablespoons (2 ounces) unsalted butter, melted

¼ teaspoon salt

EQUIPMENT

Baking sheet

2-quart baking dish, about 2 inches deep

✳ **GOOD TO KNOW**

Freestone peaches are easier to pit than clingstones—check with your grocer or vendor.

Peaches vary considerably in sweetness, hence the range of sugar. If in doubt, go easy on the sugar. You can taste the hot peaches and, if necessary, stir in more sugar before you spoon on the topping! So no worries.

✳ **VARIATIONS**

Lemon-Scented Peach Crisp

Toss the grated zest and juice of 1 medium lemon with the peaches.

Peach Crisp with Dried Fruit

Toss ½ cup (2.5 ounces) raisins or diced dried fruit with the peaches.

Peach Crisp with Candied Ginger

Toss 2 tablespoons chopped crystallized ginger with the peaches.

DIRECTIONS

Position a rack in the lower third of the oven and preheat the oven to 350°F. Line the baking sheet with parchment paper or foil.

TO MAKE THE FILLING Mix the peaches with the flour, sugar, and cinnamon in the baking dish. Put on the lined baking sheet, to catch any drips, and bake for 25 to 30 minutes, until the mixture is bubbling at the edges.

MEANWHILE, TO MAKE THE TOPPING Thoroughly mix all the ingredients in a medium bowl.

When the filling is ready, drop heaping tablespoonfuls of the topping all over the filling. Turn the heat up to 400°F and bake for 15 to 20 more minutes, until the filling is bubbling vigorously in the center and the topping is browned. Serve hot, warm, or at room temperature.

✳ MORE VARIATIONS

Spicy Peach Crisp

Mix ¼ teaspoon ground nutmeg or cardamom with the peaches.

Fig Crisp

A little balsamic vinegar wakes up the flavor of ripe figs. This crisp is good with or without the cinnamon or other spice.

Substitute 1 pound ripe figs, quartered or halved, depending on size, for the peaches. Use only ¼ cup sugar, and, if desired, replace the cinnamon with ¼ teaspoon ground cardamom for something a little more exotic. Add 1 tablespoon balsamic vinegar (the inexpensive kind is fine) to the filling.

Nectarine Crisp

Substitute nectarines for the peaches and add ½ cup (2.5 ounces) chopped dried apricots to the filling.

APPLE BROWN BETTY REDUX

Apple brown Betty is a very old-fashioned dessert. Early recipes were made with a bread-crumb topping; my mother made a version with cornflakes in the 1950s. This one is updated but still in keeping with the original spirit of convenience: the topping is a mixture of Ritz or saltine crackers with melted butter and spices. You will be surprised at how delicately crisp it is and how appealingly the salted crackers play against the sweet fruit. One might conclude that graham crackers would also make a great topping here, but one would be all wrong about that! Cover and refrigerate any leftovers. Try some for breakfast with a scoop of Greek yogurt.

Serves 6

INGREDIENTS

1¼ pounds firm, flavorful apples (such as Red Delicious, Granny Smith, pippins, Pink Lady, Sierra Beauty, or Braeburn), peeled, cored, and cut into 1- to 1½-inch chunks (4 cups)

½ cup (2.5 ounces) raisins or dried cranberries (optional)

2 tablespoons fresh lemon juice (use 3 tablespoons if the apples are not tart)

⅔ cup (4.625 ounces) sugar

1 cup (about 2 ounces) crushed Ritz or saltine crackers

4 tablespoons (2 ounces) unsalted butter, melted

1 teaspoon ground cinnamon

½ teaspoon ground nutmeg

EQUIPMENT

Baking sheet

1½-quart baking dish, about 2 inches deep, or a 10-inch glass or ceramic pie plate

✳ VARIATIONS

Pear and Cranberry Betty (shown at right)

Substitute cubed unpeeled pears for the apples and use the dried cranberries. Bartlett or Anjou pears are great; Boscs taste good but remain rather firm.

Plum Betty

Substitute cubed ripe plums (not prune plums) for the apples.

DIRECTIONS

Position a rack in the lower third of the oven and preheat the oven to 350°F. Line the baking sheet with parchment paper or foil.

Toss the apples, raisins or cranberries, if using, and lemon juice together in the baking dish or pie plate. Set aside.

Mix the sugar and crushed crackers in a bowl. Remove ⅓ cup of the mixture and toss it with the apples in the baking dish. Put on the lined baking sheet, to catch any drips, and bake for 25 to 30 minutes, until the mixture is bubbling at the edges.

Meanwhile, add the melted butter, cinnamon, and nutmeg to the remaining cracker mixture and mix well.

When the filling is ready, spoon the topping evenly over the fruit. Turn the heat up to 400°F and bake for 15 to 20 more minutes, until the filling is bubbling vigorously in the center and the topping is browned.

Serve the Betty hot, warm, at room temperature, or even cold.

MAYA'S LEMON-SCENTED APPLE UPSIDE-DOWN CAKE

From my colleague and frequent collaborator Maya Klein, here's a lovely light upside-down cake bright with fruit flavor and just enough buttery caramel goop. Serve with whipped cream or vanilla ice cream or lemon sorbet (try mango sorbet with the pineapple variation).

Serves 6 to 8

INGREDIENTS

1 lemon

12 tablespoons (6 ounces) unsalted butter, softened

½ cup (3.5 ounces) firmly packed light brown sugar

½ teaspoon ground cinnamon

1 large apple

1 cup (7 ounces) granulated sugar

2 large eggs, separated

1 teaspoon pure vanilla extract

2 teaspoons baking powder

¼ teaspoon salt

1½ cups (6.75 ounces) unbleached all-purpose flour

½ cup plain yogurt

EQUIPMENT

Microplane zester

9-inch round cake pan

Electric mixer

DIRECTIONS

Position a rack in the lower third of the oven and preheat the oven to 350°F.

Grate 1 teaspoon zest from the lemon into a medium bowl. Juice the lemon into a small bowl. Set aside.

Smear 4 tablespoons of the butter over the bottom of the cake pan, using the back of a spoon. Sprinkle the brown sugar and cinnamon evenly over the butter.

Peel, quarter, and core the apple, then cut into ¼-inch-thick slices. Toss the slices gently with the lemon juice. Arrange the apple slices in one even layer in the cake pan, covering all or most of the brown sugar. Sprinkle up to 1 tablespoon of any leftover lemon juice over the apple slices; set aside.

Put the remaining 8 tablespoons butter, the granulated sugar, and lemon zest in a medium bowl and beat with the mixer at high speed until the mixture is lighter in color and fluffy, 2 to 3 minutes. Add the egg yolks and vanilla and beat until well blended. Add the baking powder and salt and mix until blended. Add ⅓ cup of the flour and mix just until incorporated, then mix in the remaining flour. The mixture will be very stiff. Add the yogurt and the (unbeaten) egg whites and mix just until smooth.

Scrape the batter over the apples and spread it evenly. Bake for 35 to 40 minutes, until a tooth-pick inserted in the center of the cake comes out clean. Let the cake rest for 5 minutes, then invert it onto a plate to cool. If some of the apples stick to the pan, use a spatula to transfer them (or it) back onto the cake; the gooey brown sugar sauce will cover all sins here.

Serve warm or at room temperature. Refrigerate leftovers for up to 3 days; rewarm slices in the microwave for about 10 seconds.

✳ VARIATION

Pineapple Upside-Down Cake (shown at right)

Substitute ¼ fresh pineapple, peeled, cored, and cut into ¼-inch-thick slices (if you cut round slices, cut them into wedges), for the apple. If you like, substitute dark brown sugar or light or dark muscovado sugar for the light brown sugar.

✳ GOOD TO KNOW

If you hate to wrestle with a whole pineapple, look for peeled and cored fresh pineapple in better supermarkets.

SAUCY CRANBERRY MAPLE PUDDING CAKE

Crusty but tender and buttery cornmeal cake over juicy, tart cranberries in maple syrup is not quite pudding and not quite cake. Whipped cream or vanilla ice cream is a perfect topper, but the pudding is addictive on its own. Reheat any leftovers in the microwave.

Serves 6

INGREDIENTS

FOR THE FILLING

2½ cups (10 ounces) fresh or frozen, thawed cranberries

⅓ cup plus 1 tablespoon maple syrup (Grade B or Grade A dark amber is fine)

¼ cup water

FOR THE TOPPING

⅔ cup (3 ounces) unbleached all-purpose flour

⅓ cup (1.5 ounces) fine or medium-grind cornmeal

1½ teaspoons baking powder

½ teaspoon salt

1 large egg

½ cup whole milk

8 tablespoons (4 ounces) unsalted butter, melted and still warm

1 teaspoon pure vanilla extract

Lightly Sweetened Whipped Cream (page 130) or vanilla ice cream (optional)

EQUIPMENT

2-quart baking dish about 2 inches deep, or a 10-inch glass or ceramic pie plate

Electric mixer

DIRECTIONS

Position a rack in the center of the oven and preheat the oven to 400°F. Butter the baking dish or pie plate.

TO MAKE THE FILLING Combine the cranberries, maple syrup, and water in a medium saucepan, bring to a simmer, and cook for 3 minutes.

Transfer ½ cup of the berries, with some juice, to a small bowl and set aside. Pour the remaining berries and juice into the baking dish and set in the oven to heat for about 5 minutes while you make the topping.

TO MAKE THE TOPPING Whisk the flour, cornmeal, baking powder, and salt in a medium bowl.

Whisk the egg, milk, butter, and vanilla in another medium bowl. Add the flour mixture and whisk just until blended. Remove the baking dish from the oven and scrape the batter over the berries (without necessarily covering them all completely). Spoon the reserved berries and juice randomly over the batter.

Bake for 15 to 20 minutes, until the cornmeal topping is golden brown, feels crusty, and springs back when you press it with your fingers. Cool the pudding for 5 minutes or so before serving plain or with whipped cream or vanilla ice cream, if desired.

BERRY COBBLER

The topping is a simple recipe for cream scones made with some cornmeal for flavor and crunch. Use a single type of berry or a medley. Serve with ice cream, whipped cream, or crème fraîche, if you like.

Serves 6

INGREDIENTS

FOR THE FILLING

6 cups (about 2 pounds) mixed berries—raspberries, blackberries, blueberries, huckleberries, and/or olallieberries

3 tablespoons unbleached all-purpose flour

¾ cup (5.25 ounces) sugar

FOR THE TOPPING

½ cup (2.25 ounces) unbleached all-purpose flour

½ cup (2.33 ounces) fine or medium-grind cornmeal

3 tablespoons sugar

1½ teaspoons baking powder

½ teaspoon salt

¾ cup heavy cream

EQUIPMENT

Baking sheet

2-quart baking dish, about 2 inches deep

DIRECTIONS

Position a rack in the lower third of the oven and preheat the oven to 350°F. Line the baking sheet with parchment paper or foil.

Continued

Continued

* **GOOD TO KNOW**

Mixing the filling right in the baking dish saves time and cleanup.

* **VARIATION**

Plum Cobbler

Substitute 2½ pounds plums (not prune plums), halved, pitted, and cut into 1½-inch chunks (6 cups) for the berries.

TO MAKE THE FILLING Mix the berries with the flour and sugar in the baking dish. Put on the lined baking sheet, to catch any drips, and bake for 25 to 30 minutes, until the mixture is bubbling at the edges.

MEANWHILE, TO MAKE THE TOPPING Mix the flour, cornmeal, sugar, baking powder, and salt together with a whisk in a medium bowl. Add about half of the cream, give a few stirs, and then push the mixture to one side of the bowl. Pour the remaining cream into the bottom of the bowl and mix gently until all of the flour and cornmeal are moistened.

When the filling is ready, use two forks to drop craggy-looking lumps of dough (each about a heaping tablespoon) all over the top of the fruit. Turn the heat up to 400°F and bake for 10 to 15 more minutes, until the filling is bubbling vigorously in the center and the topping is browned. Serve the cobbler hot, warm, or at room temperature.

Cover and refrigerate any leftovers. The cobbler topping hardens unappealingly when it is chilled, so reheat in a microwave or a 350°F oven just until the topping softens, or until the fruit is as hot as you like.

BLUEBERRY CORNMEAL COBBLER

Think blueberry cornmeal muffin turned inside out: that is, lots of juicy berries with just enough crusty cornmeal topping.

Serves 6

INGREDIENTS

FOR THE FILLING

6 cups (about 2 pounds) blueberries

3 tablespoons fresh lemon juice

¾ cup (5.25 ounces) sugar

3 tablespoons unbleached all-purpose flour

FOR THE TOPPING

½ cup (2.25 ounces) unbleached all-purpose flour

½ cup (2.33 ounces) fine or medium-grind cornmeal

2 tablespoons sugar

½ teaspoon baking powder

¼ teaspoon baking soda

¼ teaspoon salt

4 tablespoons (2 ounces) unsalted butter, melted

½ cup buttermilk or plain yogurt

EQUIPMENT

Baking sheet

2-quart baking dish, about 2 inches deep

✳ VARIATION

You can substitute the topping for Berry Cobbler (page 75), which calls for heavy cream rather than yogurt or buttermilk, no butter, a bit more sugar, and no baking soda.

DIRECTIONS

Position a rack in the lower third of the oven and preheat the oven to 350°F. Line the baking sheet with parchment paper or foil.

TO MAKE THE FILLING Mix the berries with the lemon juice, sugar, and flour in the baking dish. Put on the lined baking sheet to catch any drips, and bake for 25 to 30 minutes, until the mixture is bubbling at the edges.

MEANWHILE, TO MAKE THE TOPPING Mix the flour, cornmeal, sugar, baking powder, baking soda, and salt together with a whisk in a medium bowl.

Mix the melted butter with the buttermilk or yogurt in another medium bowl. Add the dry ingredients all at once and mix with a rubber spatula only until all the ingredients are uniformly moist; do not overmix.

When the filling is ready, use two forks to drop craggy-looking lumps of dough (each about a heaping tablespoon) all over the top of the fruit. Turn the heat up to 400°F and bake for 15 to 20 more minutes, until the filling is bubbling vigorously in the center and the topping is browned. Serve the cobbler hot, warm, or at room temperature.

Cover and refrigerate any leftovers. The cobbler topping hardens unappealingly when it is chilled, so reheat in a microwave or a 350°F oven just until the topping softens, or until the fruit is as hot as you like.

SPARKLING FRUIT SAUCES

Whether chunky or pureed, fruit sauces add gorgeous color and a brilliant contrast of flavor and texture to almost any dessert you can name. Some are substantial enough to eat in a bowl with a spoon! All are easy to make and keep well.

MAPLE CRANBERRY SAUCE

Cranberries are tart, tangy, flavorful, and gorgeously red. And they are fresh and ripe when other berries are out of season. Why do we only serve them with the Thanksgiving turkey? Simmer them in maple syrup for less than ten minutes and you'll have a dynamite sauce for vanilla ice cream and a spectacular inspiration for myriad other sweets. Flavor the sauce with a piece of vanilla bean, a strip of orange zest, or crystallized ginger and you'll have a repertoire of sauces. Serve with Buttermilk Panna Cotta (page 106); Sour Cream Soufflés (page 123); scones and Devonshire cream, crème fraîche, or mascarpone; or a toasted bagel with cream cheese. Or spoon over fromage blanc, ricotta, cottage cheese, or any fresh creamy-style cheese; a scoop of vanilla ice cream (and add a shot of bourbon); or a slice of One-Bowl Vanilla Cake (page 222) or store-bought sponge cake drizzled with rum and orange juice and topped with a dollop of crème fraîche or whipped cream.

Makes 1 cup

⅔ cup maple syrup (Grade B is fine)
1½ cups (6 ounces) fresh or frozen, thawed cranberries
¼ cup water, cranberry juice, or other fruit juice

Combine the syrup, berries, and water or juice in a medium saucepan and bring to a simmer. Cover the pan, reduce the heat slightly, and simmer for 8 to 10 minutes, stirring occasionally, until the berries have collapsed and the syrup around them is deep red.

The sauce will thicken and seem even chunkier as it cools. For a less chunky sauce, press half through a medium-fine-mesh strainer into a bowl with the back of a spoon until you have only a little fibrous material left in the strainer. Scrape the sauce clinging to the underside of the strainer into the bowl, and discard the material left in the strainer. Stir in the rest of the sauce.

Serve the sauce hot or warm. Or let cool, cover, and refrigerate until needed. The sauce keeps in a covered container in the refrigerator for at least 2 weeks. Reheat to serve.

SAUCE BIJOUX

A longtime favorite, this sparkling, ruby-red raw cranberry sauce is a gorgeous and suitably tangy alternative to fresh raspberry puree. You can flavor it to taste with a little orange liqueur and grated orange or lemon zest, a pinch of ground cinnamon, or what you will.

Makes about 2 cups

3 cups (12 ounces) fresh or frozen, thawed cranberries
¾ cup (5.25 ounces) sugar
¾ cup seedless or strained raspberry preserves, or to taste

Combine the cranberries with the sugar in a food processor and puree as finely as possible.

Use a rubber spatula or the back of a spoon to press the puree through a medium-fine-mesh strainer into a bowl to remove the toughest skins until you have only about ⅓ cup pulp and skins left in the strainer. Scrape the sauce clinging to the underside of the strainer into the bowl and discard the pulp. Stir the raspberry preserves into the puree. Taste, and adjust the sweetness with more preserves, if you like. The sauce keeps in a covered container in the refrigerator for at least 3 weeks, or it can be frozen for up to 6 months.

HANNAH'S BERRIES

Hannah Hoffman helps me with recipe testing and ideas. When she needs dessert "right now," she empties a bag of frozen berries into a saucepan, brings the berries to a boil, then ladles them over vanilla ice cream in a soup bowl and garnishes it with torn mint leaves from the garden. This bowl of fragrant pleasure is best enjoyed in pajamas. You can dress up her secret dessert for company by serving it in a large brandy snifter to capture the aromas and make it pretty. Tip: buy individually frozen (IQF) unsweetened berries, not a block of frozen sweetened berries.

SAUCY BERRIES

The combination of bright fresh-fruit flavor and the deeper jammy notes from the cooked berries makes this the sauce that you will spoon over a slice of Sour Cream and Brown Sugar Tart (page 147) or ricotta soufflés, or around a quivery Buttermilk Panna Cotta (page 106). But when you have nothing to sauce, scoop this berry bliss into a bowl and eat it with a generous spoonful of crème fraîche or fresh cheese. You can flavor the berries toward the end of cooking with pinches of ground cinnamon or cardamom to taste. Or add

a 4-inch sprig of fresh thyme, tarragon, lemon verbena, or mint to the pan along with the berries.

Makes 2 cups

3 cups fresh blackberries, raspberries, olallieberries, or other berries, or a combination

2 tablespoons sugar, or to taste

2 tablespoons water or red wine

A few drops of fresh lemon juice

Put one-third to one-half of the berries in a medium saucepan with the sugar and water or wine and cook over medium heat, covered, until the berries release their juices, 2 to 3 minutes. Stir, cover, and continue to cook until the berries are collapsed and the juices are sweet and rich and syrupy.

Fold in the remaining berries and just warm them through. Taste, and adjust the flavor with sugar if necessary and a few drops of lemon juice. Serve warm or chilled. The sauce keeps in a covered container in the refrigerator for 3 to 4 days.

RASPBERRY BLACKBERRY PUREE

Fresh uncooked berry puree is light, bright, and tangy—and sometimes it needs a little extra sweetness. You can always add sugar to taste, but sweetening with berry preserves (made from the same or complementary berries) deepens the

flavor and adds a little complexity to the berry flavor without overwhelming the sparkly flavor of the fruit. If you love the combination of ultra-rich dark chocolate desserts with berry sauce, this is the one to serve with My Favorite Flourless Chocolate Cake (page 191).

Makes about 1½ cups

2 cups (12 ounces) fresh or frozen unsweetened (IQF) raspberries and blackberries

¼ cup raspberry or blackberry preserves or jam, or to taste

If the berries are frozen, defrost them in a medium-fine-mesh strainer set over a bowl to capture their juice.

Puree the berries in a food processor or a blender. Push through the strainer into a bowl to remove the seeds. Stir in the preserves. Taste, and adjust the sweetness by adding more jam if necessary. If using frozen berries, add a little of the reserved juice to taste and/or to thin the sauce if desired. Cover and refrigerate until chilled. The sauce keeps in a covered container in the refrigerator for several days, or it can be frozen for up to 3 months.

DESSERT CHUTNEY

This is spicy and a little tart and quite fun as a concept. Make it once, and you'll make it again to taste, without even opening the book. Dessert Chutney is a perfect accompaniment for Creamy, Dreamy Rice Pudding (page 102) or ice cream. I also love it with mascarpone. And leftovers can be served as traditional chutney, with roasted, braised, or grilled meats! Red apples make a particularly pretty chutney.

Makes 3 cups

INGREDIENTS

1 pound apples or firm pears, halved, cored, and coarsely chopped (4 cups)

1 cup (5 ounces) dark or golden raisins, or a mix

½ teaspoon ground cloves

½ teaspoon ground ginger

½ teaspoon ground allspice

¼ cup apple cider vinegar or fresh lime juice (from 2 to 3 limes)

2 tablespoons chopped crystallized ginger

½ cup (3.5 ounces) firmly packed brown sugar

DIRECTIONS

Combine all the ingredients in a medium saucepan and bring to a simmer over medium heat. Cover, reduce the heat, and simmer for 10 minutes, stirring gently once or twice, or until the fruit is just tender. Serve at room temperature or chilled. The chutney keeps in a covered container in the refrigerator for at least a week.

❋ VARIATIONS

Pineapple Dessert Chutney

This is intense, thus best over a rich ice cream such as coconut or mango.

Substitute chopped fresh pineapple for the apples or pears. Use only ¼ teaspoon cloves, and add ¼ teaspoon red pepper flakes. Uncover the pan during the last 3 to 4 minutes of simmering to evaporate excess liquid.

Dessert Crostini

Toast buttered baguette slices, spread them with either chutney, and serve with ice cream.

❋ GOOD TO KNOW

You can substitute diced dried fruits, such as apricots, pears, or figs, for the raisins.

PLUMS IN BRANDIED COFFEE SYRUP

These are heavenly—rich tasting with a velvety texture. Serve with a little mascarpone or with mini scoops of vanilla ice cream after an elegant meal. Or spoon them around a serving of Fresh Ginger Gingerbread (page 213).

Serves 4 to 6

INGREDIENTS

2 cups strong coffee (not espresso)

1 cup (7 ounces) sugar, or more to taste

1 teaspoon pure vanilla extract

2 tablespoons brandy

1¾ to 2 pounds prune plums, halved and pitted (5 to 6 cups)

DIRECTIONS

Combine all the ingredients in a medium saucepan and bring to a simmer. Cover and simmer for 5 to 10 minutes, turning the plums gently once or twice, until just tender. Taste and add sugar to balance the flavor if necessary. Serve hot, warm, or chilled. The plums keep in the refrigerator for at least a week.

✳ GOOD TO KNOW
French and Italian Plums

These are oval plums often called prune plums. Their flavor is mellow and medium sweet rather than tart and sweet.

✳ TIP

Make the coffee a little stronger than you usually drink it *unless* your daily brew is pretty strong already.

PUDDING PLEASURE

Smooth, silky, saucy, creamy, dreamy . . . Pudding is all of this and more. It is the perfect comfy-elegant company dessert. Add a touch of salt, a sprinkle of black pepper, or a slather of an exotic whipped cream for a contemporary vibe, or keep it plain and soulful. Here you'll find old-school chocolate pudding dialed up and worthy of today's great chocolates and cocoas; chocolate mousses old and new; flans with a difference; ethereal rice pudding; gooey, saucy bread pudding; and panna cotta to swoon over. Here too are a handful of recipes for that iconic culinary nemesis, the soufflé, made completely doable (and do-ahead-able), so any cook can succeed.

MY CHOCOLATE PUDDING 3.0

Every cook needs a good chocolate pudding recipe. After a short-lived infatuation with an egg-enriched pudding, I've returned to my first love. This simple pudding is reliable and quite spectacular when made with superb cocoa and great chocolate. Serve unadorned or with poured cream (as shown in the photograph on page 86), whipped cream, or crème fraîche. And if you love this pudding as I do, you'll like it dressed up for company in bittersweet Chocolate Pudding Pie (page 139) and in its extra-thick incarnation, with cinnamon toast; see the variation.

Serves 6 to 8

INGREDIENTS

⅓ cup (2.33 ounces) sugar

⅓ cup (1 ounce) unsweetened cocoa powder, preferably natural

2 tablespoons cornstarch

⅛ teaspoon salt

1¾ cups whole milk

¼ cup heavy cream

3 to 4 ounces bittersweet chocolate (use the lesser amount for chocolate in the 66% to 70% cacao range and the full 4 ounces for chocolate closer to 60%), very finely chopped

1 teaspoon pure vanilla extract

1 tablespoon dark rum (optional)

FOR THE TOPPING (OPTIONAL)

1 cup heavy cream, for pouring, or Lightly Sweetened Whipped Cream (page 130) or crème fraîche

EQUIPMENT

Six 4-ounce custard cups or ramekins or 8 smaller cups

✳ GOOD TO KNOW

Puddings are elegant served in demitasses with whipped cream or comfy and casual served in small canning jars with pouring cream.

DIRECTIONS

Whisk the sugar, cocoa, cornstarch, and salt together in a heavy medium saucepan. Add about 3 tablespoons of the milk and whisk to form a smooth paste. Whisk in the remaining milk and the cream. Using a silicone spatula or a wooden spoon, stir the mixture constantly over medium heat, scraping the bottom, sides, and corners of the pan, until the pudding thickens and begins to bubble at the edges, about 5 minutes. Continue to cook and stir for 1 minute, then add the chocolate and stir briskly until the chocolate is melted and the pudding is smooth, about 30 seconds longer. Remove from the heat and stir in the vanilla and rum, if using.

Divide the pudding among the cups or ramekins. (I love skin on pudding, so I wouldn't dream of pressing a piece of plastic wrap on the surface for later removal, and you needn't tell me if you do.) Serve warm or at room temperature or chilled. The pudding can be covered and refrigerated for up to 3 days.

Serve with poured cream or whipped cream or crème fraîche, if desired.

✴ VARIATION

Extra-Thick Chocolate Pudding with Cinnamon Toast

A little sleight of hand produces a richer and stiffer pudding, so thick it's served with an ice cream scoop. Serve with knives so guests can spread it on their cinnamon toast, and have extra cinnamon toast on hand for seconds.

Reduce the sugar to 3 tablespoons. Use 1½ cups whole milk and ½ cup heavy cream. Increase the chocolate to 5 ounces and use one with up to but no more than 62% cacao. Make as directed, scrape into a bowl, and chill. Use an ice cream scoop to serve on plates, with warm Spice-Drawer Cinnamon Toast (page 28).

BILL'S FOOD-PROCESSOR CHOCOLATE MOUSSE

Executive chef at Draeger's Cooking School in San Mateo, California, Bill Hutton is the guy who makes my life easy by seeing that every bit of my prep is done for me when I teach. I love the guy, and I love his mousse. No eggs in this super-creamy version. And it sets up quickly, so you can *almost* serve it right after you make it. Bill grinds a little black pepper on top for extra chocolate excitement.

Serves 6

INGREDIENTS

7 ounces semisweet or bittersweet chocolate (not more than 62% cacao), coarsely chopped

2 tablespoons flavorless vegetable oil

1 tablespoon red wine or liqueur

1 tablespoon pure vanilla extract

⅓ cup milk or water

2 tablespoons sugar

Pinch of kosher or sea salt

1 cup heavy cream

Freshly ground black pepper (optional)

EQUIPMENT

Food processor

Electric mixer (optional)

6 dessert glasses or cups

✷ GOOD TO KNOW

You can make a chocolate mousse pie by substituting Bill's mousse for the filling in Chocolate Pudding Pie (page 139) or Milk Chocolate Pudding Pie with Salted Peanut Crust (page 137).

DIRECTIONS

Process the chocolate in the food processor until very finely ground; leave it in the processor bowl.

Combine the oil, wine, and vanilla in a small cup.

Bring the milk or water, sugar, and salt to a simmer in a small saucepan, stirring to dissolve the sugar. Immediately, with the processor running, pour the hot milk through the feed tube, processing for 15 to 20 seconds, or until the chocolate is melted. Add the oil mixture and process for 5 to 10 seconds, until thoroughly blended. Scrape the mixture into a large bowl and let cool for 5 to 10 minutes (the chocolate should not be warm when the cream is added).

Beat the cream until it holds a very soft shape (not even close to stiff). Fold one-third of the cream into the chocolate to lighten it. Fold in the remaining cream just until blended. Immediately divide the mousse among the dessert glasses. Refrigerate until serving. The mousse keeps for 2 days in the refrigerator. Grind a little black pepper over each serving, if desired.

✳ TIP

For the smoothest possible mousse, stop folding the moment the cream is incorporated into the chocolate, and immediately scoop it into the glasses.

OLD-SCHOOL FRENCH CHOCOLATE MOUSSE 2.0

Once upon a time, French chocolate mousse was made with raw eggs. I've revised this classic recipe so that the eggs are heated enough to be safe. It's still simple to make, and to me it tastes like Paris!

Serves 6 to 8

INGREDIENTS

4 ounces bittersweet or semisweet chocolate (no more than 62% cacao), chopped into small pieces

⅓ cup heavy cream

1 tablespoon brandy, rum, or liqueur (optional)

2 large eggs, at room temperature

2 tablespoons sugar

Pinch of salt

1 tablespoon water

Lightly Sweetened Whipped Cream (page 130)

EQUIPMENT

Instant-read thermometer

Electric mixer

Six to eight 4- to 5-ounce ramekins or dessert cups

DIRECTIONS

Put the chocolate and cream in a medium heatproof bowl, preferably stainless steel, set it in a wide skillet of barely simmering water (see Melting Chocolate My Way, page 97), and stir frequently until the chocolate is completely melted and smooth. Remove the bowl from the skillet, stir in the brandy, rum, or liqueur, if using, and set aside.

Continued

Continued

✳ TIP

For the best taste and texture, be sure to choose chocolate that does not exceed the cacao percentage called for. For more about cacao percentages, see the Mini Chocolate Tutorial, on page 97.

Whisk the eggs with the sugar and salt in a medium heatproof bowl, preferably stainless steel, just until well blended but not at all foamy. Whisk in the water. Set the bowl in the skillet of barely simmering water and heat, stirring the eggs constantly with a silicone spatula, sweeping the bottom and sides of the bowl, to prevent them from scrambling, until they register 160°F on the thermometer. Remove the bowl from the skillet.

With the electric mixer, beat the eggs at high speed for 3 to 4 minutes, until they have a texture like softly whipped cream.

Fold one-quarter of the eggs into the chocolate, then scrape the chocolate mixture over the whipped eggs and fold just until evenly incorporated.

Divide the mousse among the ramekins and chill for at least 1 hour, or until set; the mousse can be refrigerated for up to a day.

Top each mousse with a dollop of whipped cream and serve.

CHOCOLATE MARQUISE

Chocolate mousse enriched with butter is called a marquise. Choose a distinctive chocolate you like to eat, because it is all about the chocolate.

Serves 8 to 10

INGREDIENTS

8 ounces bittersweet or semisweet chocolate (no more than 62% cacao), coarsely chopped

8 tablespoons (4 ounces) unsalted butter

4 large eggs, at room temperature

¼ cup (1.75 ounces) sugar

Pinch of salt

¼ cup water

Lightly Sweetened Whipped Cream (page 130)

EQUIPMENT

Instant-read thermometer

Electric mixer

8 to 10 dessert bowls or martini glasses

DIRECTIONS

Put the chocolate and butter in a medium heatproof bowl, preferably stainless steel, set it in a wide skillet of barely simmering water (see Melting Chocolate My Way, page 97), and stir frequently until the mixture is completely melted and smooth. Remove the bowl from the skillet and set aside.

Whisk the eggs with the sugar and salt in a medium heatproof bowl, preferably stainless steel, just until well blended but not at all foamy. Whisk in the water. Set the bowl in the skillet of barely simmering water and heat, stirring the eggs constantly with a silicone spatula, sweeping

* **GOOD TO KNOW**

This mousse sets up firm enough to use as a pie filling. You can substitute it for the filling of either Chocolate Pudding Pie (page 139) or Milk Chocolate Pudding Pie with Salted Peanut Crust (page 137).

the bottom and sides of the bowl, to prevent them from scrambling, until they register 160°F on the thermometer. Remove the bowl from the skillet.

With the electric mixer, beat the eggs at high speed for 3 to 4 minutes, until they have a texture like softly whipped cream.

Fold one-quarter of the eggs into the chocolate, then fold in half the remaining eggs until nearly blended. Add the rest of the eggs and fold just until evenly incorporated.

Immediately, before the mousse begins to set, divide it among the dessert dishes. Refrigerate for at least 1 hour, or until set. The mousse can be refrigerated for up to a day.

Top each mousse with a dollop of whipped cream and serve.

MINI CHOCOLATE TUTORIAL

Unless otherwise noted, the recipes in this book turn out beautifully with common supermarket brands of chocolate, as long as they are the type of chocolate, and percentage of cacao, called for in the recipe.

HOW TO CHOOSE BITTERSWEET AND SEMISWEET CHOCOLATES

Bittersweet and semisweet chocolates come in such a wide range of cacao percentages that they are not always interchangeable. When chocolate is melted and blended into a dough or a batter, the cacao percentage of the chocolate affects not only the flavor and sweetness of the finished product but also its texture and moistness. Bottom line? Choose chocolate within the range of cacao content called for.

HOW TO CHOOSE CHOCOLATE CHIPS AND CHUNKS

When chocolate chips or chunks are added intact to a recipe, their cacao content will affect the flavor but not the texture of your results. So you can choose chips or chunks with any cacao percentage that you like, keeping in mind that the higher the cacao percentage, the stronger and more bittersweet the flavor. See Ingredients (page 270) for more about chocolate chips.

HOW AND WHY TO KEEP CHOCOLATE DRY

Chocolate to be melted alone (without butter or cream or another ingredient) should be kept thoroughly dry, because even a small amount of moisture can cause the chocolate to tighten, or "seize," instead of melting smoothly. Chop the chocolate on a dry board with a dry knife, and melt in a dry bowl.

MELTING CHOCOLATE MY WAY

Rather than using a double boiler, as all cooks are taught to do, I melt chocolate in a stainless steel bowl set directly in a skillet of barely simmering water (aka an open water bath) that is several inches wider than the bowl, to prevent the edges of the bowl from getting too hot to touch. The specific steps are given in each recipe (they can vary depending on what type of chocolate you are melting), so you don't really have to read any further unless you are curious about why the bath is less likely to scorch chocolate—and more flexible—than a double boiler.

Continued

With either method, you are meant to see that the water barely simmers and to stir the chocolate from time to time. But the water in a double boiler is out of sight, and covered, thus more likely to boil without your even noticing. So, unless you are obsessively careful, your chocolate will be sitting over a closed chamber of steam that is far hotter than boiling water. And the common technique of creating a make-shift double boiler by setting a bowl over a pot of water creates additional risk: the sides and rim of the bowl (and thus the chocolate) above the pot are exposed to scorching heat from the burner flame licking up the sides of the pan.

The open water bath is better: you can turn the heat down or off if you see the water bubbling too much. Although the bowl sits on the bottom of the skillet, there is actually a thin film of water between the bowl and the pan that buffers the heat. The water in the open bath can never exceed the temperature of boiling water, and it is likely to be cooler since it is easier to monitor. And the sides of the bowl don't get too hot, because they don't extend beyond the sides of the bath.

Meanwhile, the open bath lets you melt the chocolate in the size bowl needed: a small bowl for a couple of ounces of chocolate, a large bowl if the recipe calls for mixing the rest of the ingredients into the chocolate bowl. A double boiler limits you to using its top pan, or a bowl at least wide enough to set over a pot.

Coda: if you still like your double boiler, at least stop worrying about whether the container of chocolate touches the water beneath it!

HOW TO MELT CHOCOLATE IN A MICROWAVE

Chop semisweet or bittersweet chocolate into pieces about the size of almonds; chop milk chocolate or white chocolate very fine. Put the chocolate in a microwave-safe container and heat dark chocolate on medium (50%) power, milk and white chocolate on low (30%, or defrost). Start with 1 to 2 minutes for amounts up to 3 ounces, or 3 minutes for larger amounts. Then, even if most of the chocolate is unmelted, stir it well before microwaving in increments of 5 to 15 seconds or more, depending on how much of the chocolate is left unmelted each time, stirring after each one. Be conservative: the goal is to make the chocolate warm, not hot.

BAKED HOT CHOCOLATE PUDDING WITH THE WORKS

This dessert is a big wow, inspired by a dessert created by Jennifer Millar, pastry chef and owner of Sweet Adeline Bakeshop in Berkeley. Each guest gets a generous bowl of hot, soft, and gooey bittersweet chocolate with a slightly crusted top—something between a rich pudding and a poufy soufflé—topped with a scoop of coffee or vanilla ice cream, a drizzle of caramel sauce, and a few toasted almonds. Honestly, the bowl of hot chocolate pudding is pretty delicious on its own, or with just a generous spoonful of whipped cream.

Serves 6

INGREDIENTS

6 ounces semisweet or bittersweet chocolate (I like something around 70% cacao, but the choice is yours here), coarsely chopped

8 tablespoons (4 ounces) unsalted butter

3 large eggs

⅔ cup (4.625 ounces) sugar

Pinch of salt

6 small scoops vanilla or coffee ice cream

About ½ cup caramel sauce, store-bought or homemade (see page 25)

⅓ cup chopped toasted almonds

EQUIPMENT

Electric mixer

Six 12- to 16-ounce ramekins or ovenproof bowls

Baking sheet

Microplane zester (optional)

❋ GOOD TO KNOW

You can bake these ahead and reheat them just before serving, or you can put the batter into the bowls ahead of time and then bake just before serving.

DIRECTIONS

Position a rack in the lower third of the oven and preheat the oven to 375°F.

Put the chocolate and butter in a medium heatproof bowl, preferably stainless steel, set it in a wide skillet of barely simmering water (see Melting Chocolate My Way, page 97), and stir frequently until the mixture is completely melted and smooth. Remove the bowl from the skillet and set aside.

With the electric mixer, beat the eggs, sugar, and salt in a medium bowl at high speed until light, fluffy, and the consistency of softly whipped cream (this can take 5 to 10 minutes with a hand-held mixer). Fold one-third of the eggs into the chocolate mixture, then scrape the chocolate batter over the remaining eggs and fold until blended. Divide the batter among the ramekins or bowls. (You can cover and refrigerate the puddings to bake later in the day; remove the bowls from the fridge 30 minutes before baking.)

Place the bowls on the baking sheet and bake for 15 to 20 minutes (a little longer if the puddings were refrigerated), until the puddings are puffed, crusted, and deeply cracked but still gooey inside when tested with a toothpick. Serve immediately, or let cool, cover, and keep at room temperature for up to a day. (The puddings will sink as they cool but will puff up again if you reheat them in a preheated 375°F oven for about 10 minutes.)

To serve, top each pudding with a scoop of ice cream, a drizzle of sauce, and a sprinkling of toasted almonds.

CREAMY, DREAMY RICE PUDDING

Don't think of your mother's rice pudding, even if hers was divine. This one is light and creamy and elegant, and not too sweet. I've added nuances of flavor and fragrance from some favorite ingredients: basmati rice, cinnamon, cardamom, and saffron. Serve with Dessert Chutney (page 82) or sugared or very sweet ripe berries.

Serves 8 to 12

INGREDIENTS

4 cups whole milk

½ cup (3.5 ounces) basmati, jasmine, or other long-grain rice (not converted or instant rice)

¼ teaspoon ground cinnamon

¼ teaspoon ground cardamom

¼ teaspoon crumbled saffron threads

¼ cup (1.75 ounces) sugar

1 cup heavy cream

A cinnamon stick or pinches of ground cinnamon for garnish (optional)

DIRECTIONS

Rinse a medium saucepan with cold water and add the milk, rice, cinnamon, cardamom, and saffron and bring to a simmer. Simmer, uncovered, stirring often, for 30 minutes, or until the rice is very tender.

Stir in the sugar, let cool, and refrigerate until chilled.

Whip the cream just until it holds very soft peaks. Fold into the cold pudding just until combined. Chill before serving. Grate a little cinnamon stick over each serving or sprinkle with pinches of ground cinnamon before serving, if desired. The pudding keeps in the refrigerator for 2 to 3 days.

✳ TIP

For the perfect texture, beat the cream less than you might think you should.

✳ VARIATION

Creamy, Dreamy Vanilla Rice Pudding

Substitute a whole vanilla bean for the cinnamon, cardamom, and saffron. Remove the bean just before whipping the cream. Taste the rice, then either slice the bean lengthwise and scrape the seeds into the pudding for extra flavor, or rinse and dry the bean for another use. Proceed as directed.

COCONUT RICE PUDDING
WITH CRISPY COCONUT CHIPS

It's hard to beat the pure delicate flavor of coconut in this not-too-sweet pudding with its gorgeous toasty topping, but you can play around with it too; see the variations.

Serves 8 to 10

INGREDIENTS

FOR THE PUDDING

⅔ cup (4.625 ounces) sugar

⅔ cup (2 ounces) unsweetened shredded dried coconut

⅔ cup (4.625 ounces) short-, medium-, or long-grain rice (not converted or instant rice)

Two 14- to 15-ounce cans low-fat (also called "light") unsweetened coconut milk

One 14-ounce can regular unsweetened coconut milk

Generous ¾ teaspoon salt

½ vanilla bean, split, or 2 teaspoons pure vanilla extract

FOR THE COCONUT CHIPS

1 large egg white

3 tablespoons sugar

½ teaspoon pure vanilla extract

Pinch of salt

2½ cups (4 ounces) unsweetened coconut chips (see Ingredients, page 270)

EQUIPMENT

Baking sheet

✳ VARIATIONS

For a Latin American twist, grate a bit of cinnamon stick and fresh lime zest on top of the pudding before serving. Or dust lightly with ground cardamom or star anise or grated nutmeg. You can also add 2 to 3 tablespoons of rum with the vanilla, and serve the pudding with sautéed bananas or grilled pineapple fans.

DIRECTIONS

Position a rack in the center of the oven and preheat the oven to 300°F.

TO MAKE THE PUDDING Combine the sugar, shredded coconut, rice, coconut milk, and salt in a 3- to 4-quart heavy saucepan. If using a vanilla bean, scrape the seeds from the pod, using the tip of a paring knife, and toss into the pan, along with the pod (do not add the extract, if using, at this point). Bring to a gentle simmer, stirring, then reduce the heat until the mixture is just barely simmering and cook, partially covered, stirring frequently, until the mixture thickens to a creamy, slightly translucent pudding the consistency of loose porridge, about 1 hour.

MEANWHILE, TOAST THE COCONUT CHIPS Line the baking sheet with parchment paper. Whisk the egg white, sugar, vanilla, and salt in a medium bowl until well blended. Add the coconut, stirring and tossing until all of it is moistened. Scatter the coconut over the baking sheet.

Bake for 9 to 10 minutes, until the coconut begins to turn golden. Scrape up the coconut with a large spatula and spread it out again. Bake for another 1 to 3 minutes, watching carefully, until most of the coconut is golden, with some white patches. Let cool completely, then transfer to an airtight container to keep crisp.

When the pudding is done, fish out the pieces of vanilla pods and, when they are cool enough, scrape any remaining seeds into the pudding. (Discard the pod pieces or rinse and save them to make Vanilla Sugar, page 53.) Or stir in the vanilla extract. Scrape the pudding into a serving bowl or individual dishes.

Serve the pudding warm, at room temperature, or chilled, topped generously, at the very last minute, with coconut chips. The pudding keeps, covered, in the refrigerator for 3 to 4 days.

BUTTERMILK PANNA COTTA

Panna cotta is one of the simplest, most magnificent desserts there is. In Italy, I can't get enough of it, but in the American kitchen (including restaurants), it is often misunderstood. Panna cotta should be creamy yet ethereal on the palate. It should *never* be firm—it should be so gently set that it wobbles or even sags slightly after it's unmolded. Buttermilk Panna Cotta is luxurious and just tangy enough to wake up your palate. It loves a handful of blueberries or strawberries, plain or lightly sugared, or Saucy Berries (page 81).

Serves 6

INGREDIENTS

¼ cup water

2½ teaspoons unflavored gelatin

1½ cups heavy cream

⅓ cup (2.33 ounces) sugar

Pinch of salt

2½ cups buttermilk

EQUIPMENT

Six 6-ounce ramekins or dessert dishes

DIRECTIONS

Oil the ramekins or dishes with flavorless vegetable oil or vegetable oil spray.

Pour the water into a small bowl and sprinkle the gelatin over the surface. Set aside, without stirring, to let the gelatin soften.

Meanwhile, heat the cream, sugar, and salt in a saucepan or in a bowl in the microwave until steaming hot, stirring from time to time to dissolve the sugar. Remove from the heat, add the water and gelatin, and stir well to melt and disperse the gelatin. Cool the mixture until lukewarm.

Continued

✳ GOOD TO KNOW

3 Tips for Tender Panna Cotta

1] The contents of gelatin packets are not consistent. To avoid using too much, empty packets into a cup, then measure by scooping and leveling each teaspoon.

2] Stir the panna cotta mixture as it cools, until it starts to thicken, before pouring it into the ramekins.

3] Don't panic if the mixture actually starts to set (like Jell-O) before you've poured it into the ramekins. Set the pan in a bowl of very hot water and stir the mixture, sweeping the sides and bottom, just long enough to melt any of the mixture that started to set. Proceed as directed.

Add the buttermilk and stir thoroughly. Let stand a little longer, stirring frequently (for an especially tender panna cotta) with a rubber spatula and sweeping the sides and bottom of the bowl to prevent the mixture from setting around the edges. As soon as the mixture feels cool to the touch and is starting to thicken, divide it evenly among the ramekins or dishes (see Good to Know, page 106). Cover with plastic wrap and chill for at least 4 hours, or overnight.

Serve the panna cottas in their ramekins, or unmold them: slide a sharp paring knife around the edges of each panna cotta to detach it from the ramekin. Top it with a dessert plate or bowl and invert. Lift the ramekin slowly, at an angle, to let the panna cotta settle onto the plate. Serve cold.

✳ VARIATION
Sweet Cream Panna Cotta

This is even richer than Buttermilk Panna Cotta, but you can alter the ratio of cream to milk to make it lighter if you like.

Proceed as directed, but instead of adding buttermilk to the lukewarm mixture, add an additional 1½ cups cold heavy cream plus 1 cup whole milk.

COCONUT FLANS
WITH MUSCOVADO SUGAR SAUCE

Dark muscovado sugar is a deep mahogany color and very flavorful. It easily takes the place of the traditional caramelized sugar in these flans; all you have to do is press it into the bottom of each cup, then ladle the flan mixture on top of it. The sugar dissolves into a sauce when the flans are chilled. These are extra good with a little grated lime zest and cinnamon stick added just before serving. For old-school flans with caramelized sugar, see the variation.

Serves 8

INGREDIENTS

FOR THE SUGAR SAUCE

⅔ cup (4.625 ounces) firmly packed dark muscovado sugar

¼ teaspoon salt

FOR THE FLANS

5 large eggs

¾ cup (5.25 ounces) sugar

½ teaspoon pure vanilla extract or 1 tablespoon rum

⅛ teaspoon salt

3 cups unsweetened coconut milk (from two 14- to 15-ounce cans)

A cinnamon stick (optional)

A lime or two, preferably unsprayed or organic (optional)

EQUIPMENT

Eight 6-ounce custard cups or ramekins

Baking pan large enough to hold the custard cups with space between them

Fine-mesh strainer

Microplane zester (optional)

✳ **GOOD TO KNOW**

For the maximum amount of sauce, make the flans 12 or even 24 hours ahead to allow time for the muscovado sugar to dissolve completely.

✳ **VARIATIONS**

Sweet Cream Flans with Muscovado Sugar Sauce

Substitute 3 cups half-and-half for the coconut milk.

Caramelized Coconut Flans

Substitute ⅔ cup (4.625 ounces) granulated sugar and ⅓ cup water for the muscovado sugar and follow the procedure for lining the cups with caramel, as for Coffee Flans on page 112.

DIRECTIONS

Position a rack in the lower third of the oven and preheat the oven to 350°F. Put a kettle of water on to boil.

TO LINE THE CUPS WITH SUGAR Combine the muscovado sugar thoroughly with the salt, pinching or mashing the sugar to eliminate lumps. Divide the mixture among the custard cups or ramekins and press lightly on the sugar with another small cup to even it out and compact it. Set the cups in the baking pan.

TO MAKE THE FLANS Whisk the eggs, sugar, vanilla or rum, and salt together in a large bowl, without creating a lot of froth or bubbles.

Heat the coconut milk in a saucepan over medium heat until steaming. Gradually whisk the coconut milk into the eggs, again trying not to raise a froth. Pour the mixture through the strainer into another bowl to eliminate any bits of egg.

Ladle the flan mixture very gently into the custard cups or ramekins, disturbing the sugar as little as possible. Some of the sugar may float up, but it will eventually settle back down in the bottom. Put the baking pan in the oven, pull out the rack, and carefully pour enough boiling water into the pan to come halfway up the sides of the custard cups. Bake for 20 to 25 minutes, until the custard is just a little wobbly in the center.

Remove the pan from the oven and remove the cups with tongs. Cool on a rack for 15 minutes, then refrigerate for at least 4 hours, or preferably for 12 to 24 hours.

To serve, run a thin knife around the edges of each cup and invert the flan onto a rimmed plate or into a shallow bowl. Or, serve the flans in their cups—the sauce will be on the bottom. Either way, you can grate a little of the cinnamon stick and some lime zest over each flan before serving, if desired.

COFFEE FLANS

When you make the custard for these flans, some of the ground coffee from the cream infusion will escape the sieve and settle to make an attractive speckled sauce.

Serves 8

INGREDIENTS

FOR THE CARAMEL
⅓ cup water

⅔ cup (4.625 ounces) sugar

FOR THE FLANS
3¼ cups half-and-half

½ cup finely ground French-roast coffee beans

5 large eggs

¾ cup (5.25 ounces) sugar

½ teaspoon pure vanilla extract

⅛ teaspoon salt

EQUIPMENT

Eight 6-ounce custard cups or ramekins

Baking pan large enough to hold the custard cups with space between them

Fine-mesh strainer

DIRECTIONS

Position a rack in the lower third of the oven and preheat the oven to 350°F.

TO LINE THE CUPS WITH CARAMEL Set the custard cups or ramekins near the stove, along with a small white plate and a wooden skewer or a small knife. Pour the water into a 2- or 3-quart saucepan and set it over medium heat. Pour the sugar in a thin stream into the center

✳ **TIP**

You can significantly streamline this recipe by replacing the classic caramelized sugar lining for the cups with a simple layer of dark muscovado sugar (with a little salt), as for Coconut Flans on page 109.

of the pan to form a low mound. Don't stir, but if necessary, use your fingers to pat the sugar down until it is entirely moistened. Cover the pan and cook, without stirring, for a few minutes, until the sugar is dissolved. Uncover the pan and cook, without stirring, until the syrup begins to color slightly; swirl the pan gently if the caramel seems to be coloring unevenly.

Use the skewer or the tip of the knife to drop a bead of syrup onto the plate from time to time. When a drop of caramel looks medium-dark amber, remove the pan from the stove and quickly pour an equal quantity of caramel into each custard cup, tilting the cups to spread the caramel evenly over the bottom. Set the custard cups in the baking pan. Put a kettle of water on to boil.

TO MAKE THE FLANS Heat the half-and-half in a large saucepan over medium heat until it simmers. Remove the pan from the heat and stir in the coffee. Cover the pan and let steep for 5 minutes. Meanwhile, whisk the eggs, sugar, vanilla, and salt together in a large bowl without creating a lot of froth or bubbles. Whisk the coffee mixture into the eggs, again trying not to raise a froth. Pour the mixture through the strainer into another bowl to eliminate any bits of egg and the coffee grounds.

Ladle the flan mixture into the lined cups. Put the baking pan in the oven, pull out the rack, and carefully pour enough boiling water into the pan to come halfway up the sides of the custard cups. Bake for 20 to 25 minutes, until the custard is just a little wobbly in the center.

Remove the pan from the oven and remove the cups with tongs. Cool on a rack for 15 minutes, then refrigerate for at least 4 hours, or preferably for 12 hours, for maximum sauce.

Serve the flans in their cups, or run a thin knife around the edges of each cup and invert the flan onto a rimmed plate or into a shallow bowl.

YOGURT FOR DESSERT

Yogurt is a cook's dream for making easy improvised desserts, even for company. If you normally breakfast or snack virtuously on low-fat or nonfat yogurt, full-fat yogurt will taste properly luxurious for dessert, even though it is still much leaner than heavy cream, ice cream, mascarpone, or even sour cream. Of course you can stick with low-fat or nonfat yogurt if you prefer it. Greek yogurt has been drained of excess liquid, so it is thicker and more decadent on the tongue than regular and often less tangy. You can easily drain regular yogurt to get that thick rich "dessert" consistency too. And, if yogurt is too tangy for your taste, you can tame it by stirring in a little heavy cream and/or a little sugar or honey.

Greek or thickened yogurt invites you to compose rather than simply serve in a bowl with a spoon: arrange scoops of yogurt on plates with two or three pleasing partners—nuts, dried or fresh fruit, sweet syrups or honey, something tart and tangy, etc.—so guests can create perfect bites, scooping up the crunchy, chewy, creamy, sweet, and tart elements as they like. See Things to Do with Yogurt (opposite) for some examples of composed desserts.

HOW TO MAKE DRAINED OR THICKENED YOGURT OR YOGURT CHEESE

Line a strainer with a double or triple layer of paper towels or a paper coffee filter. Set the strainer over a bowl and fill it with plain regular yogurt. Cover and refrigerate the whole ensemble for at least a few hours, or until it has the consistency you are looking for. The longer the yogurt drains, the thicker and firmer it will be; after a couple of days it will be as thick as a fresh cheese. You can even drain Greek yogurt if you want it to be thicker: most of its excess liquid will get absorbed into the paper towels or coffee filter, so you will not see much liquid in the bottom of the bowl, but you will notice that the yogurt is thicker.

THINGS TO DO WITH YOGURT

Flavor with

- Orange juice and drops of orange flower water and a little grated orange zest with sugar or honey to taste: top with pistachios or chopped or slivered toasted almonds.

- Pure vanilla extract and sugar to taste: use as a topping on fresh or cooked fruit, cake, anything.

- Drops of rose water or orange flower water and sugar or honey to taste. Serve with pistachios or walnuts and dates.

Dollop on

- FB's Vanilla Pear and Apple Compote (page 52).

- Pears in Ginger Lemon Syrup (page 50).

- Fresh fruit of your choice.

- Fresh Ginger Gingerbread (page 213).

Use as a dip for

- Amaretti made with walnuts (page 240).

- Coconut Meringue Cookies (page 167).

- Right-Brain Nutty Butter Cookies (page 238).

- Strawberries.

Compose Greek or thickened yogurt with

- A scatter of strawberries and/or bananas and a heap of dark muscovado sugar.

- Honey or caramel sauce or a drizzle of aged balsamic vinegar, toasted pine nuts, and ripe figs. Scatter a few flakes of sea salt on top.

- Moist dates, walnuts, and candied orange peel.

- Sliced bananas or fresh figs, Honey Pistachios with Fennel (page 258), and a few flakes of sea salt.

- Honey and pistachios or walnuts, or trade the honey for sorghum syrup or a tiny bit of molasses. You can also substitute maple syrup for the honey and top with walnuts or toasted pecans.

Make

- Banana Yogurt Cream: Up to 3 hours before serving, mash large ripe bananas and then stir in an equal or greater quantity of plain Greek or thickened yogurt to taste. Sweeten with white or brown sugar, or honey if desired, and stir in pinches of ground cardamom to taste. Spoon into dessert glasses and chill or serve immediately topped with chopped pistachios or walnuts.

- Coconut Yogurt: Stir about ½ cup (1.5 ounces) unsweetened shredded dried coconut into 2 cups of plain Greek or thickened yogurt. Stir in drops of pure vanilla extract and about 2 tablespoons sugar, or more to taste. Refrigerate for at least 2 hours, or overnight to allow the coconut to rehydrate. Serve in glasses with a little cinnamon stick grated over the top.

BREAD PUDDING FROM THE PANTRY

The simplest bread pudding is no more than stale or lightly toasted bread layered in a dish with a basic custard. But with that as a model, you can make all kinds of bread puddings. Spread the bread with anything sweet and flavorful that you have on hand: various leftover jams, a canned sweetened chestnut spread, Nutella, sugar and spice, a nut butter mixed with honey, or caramel sauce or dulce de leche. You can tuck banana slices between the bread slices or add raisins or chopped dried fruit or chunks of chocolate. The custard can be made richer or leaner with fewer or more eggs or by changing the ratio of the milk and cream. Bread pudding is a cook's dream—flexible and open to ideas and flavors.

Serves 6 to 8

INGREDIENTS

7 or 8 thin slices slightly stale or very lightly toasted firm white sandwich bread (such as Pepperidge Farm or Oroweat/Arnold's Country Buttermilk or Country Potato Bread), brioche, or challah or enough baguette slices to fill the baking dish with 2 to 2½ layers (crusts can be trimmed off or left on)

5 large eggs

½ cup (3.5 ounces) sugar

⅛ teaspoon salt

1¼ cups whole milk

1¼ cups heavy cream

EQUIPMENT

8-inch square baking dish

Medium-fine-mesh strainer

Baking pan large enough to hold the baking dish with space all around it

✳ GOOD TO KNOW

For instant stale bread, toast fresh slices for 5 minutes on each side in a 325°F oven. Or set them on a rack for several hours or overnight.

DIRECTIONS

Cut or break large bread slices into 4 pieces each; leave baguette slices whole. Arrange the bread in the baking dish in one overlapping layer, with the rounded or pointed edges showing attractively.

Whisk the eggs, sugar, and salt in a medium bowl just until blended but not foamy. Gradually mix in the milk and cream.

Pour the egg mixture through the strainer into the baking dish. Cover the surface of the pudding with plastic wrap and press the bread pieces down into the egg mix. Put another baking dish or a few plates on top to submerge the bread in the egg mixture and let stand for at least 15 minutes, or until the bread has absorbed the liquid.

Position a rack in the lower third of the oven and preheat the oven to 325°F. Put a kettle of water on to boil.

Uncover the pudding and place the baking dish in the larger baking pan, then put the pan in the oven. Pull out the oven rack and pour enough boiling water into the larger pan to come halfway up the sides of the baking dish. Bake for 50 to 55 minutes, until a knife inserted in the pudding comes out free of custard. Remove the baking dish from the water bath and let cool. If not serving within 2 hours, cover and refrigerate.

Serve warm or at room temperature. Cold leftover pudding is divine, but you can also reheat it in the microwave on medium power for a few seconds.

SALTED CARAMEL BANANA BREAD PUDDINGS

Crusty golden-topped individual bread puddings with rich caramel on the bottom! Store-bought sauce spiked with a smidgen of sea salt makes these pretty puddings fast and easy, but you can use The Simplest Caramel Sauce (page 25). The custard is barely sweetened, for maximum contrast with the caramel, and the banana slices add flavor and fragrance. The puddings are cozy spooned right from their cups, or elegant unmolded, with the sauce all around.

Serves 8

INGREDIENTS

Rounded ¼ teaspoon salt

1¼ cups caramel sauce, store-bought or homemade (see page 25)

8 thin slices slightly stale or very lightly toasted firm white sandwich bread (such as Pepperidge Farm or Oroweat/Arnold's Country Buttermilk or Country Potato Bread)

2 ripe bananas

FOR THE CUSTARD

6 large eggs

2 tablespoons sugar

⅛ teaspoon salt

1 teaspoon pure vanilla extract

2 cups half-and-half

½ cup whole milk

2 tablespoons (1 ounce) unsalted butter, melted

EQUIPMENT

Eight 6-ounce ramekins or custard cups

Baking pan large enough to hold the ramekins with space between them

* **GOOD TO KNOW**

Cold puddings can be reheated in the microwave.

* **VARIATIONS**

Salted Caramel Banana Bread Puddings with Chocolate Chunks

Before pouring the egg mixture into the ramekins, divide 1 cup (6 ounces) semisweet, bittersweet, or milk chocolate chunks or chips among the ramekins, arranging them on top of and between the slices of bread and bananas.

Salted Caramel and Orange Bread Puddings

Stir the finely grated zest of 1 medium orange into the caramel sauce, along with the salt. Omit the bananas.

DIRECTIONS

Stir the salt into the caramel sauce. Butter the ramekins and spoon a generous tablespoon of the caramel into the bottom of each one. Spread a tablespoon of the remaining sauce on one side of each bread slice.

Cut the bananas on a slight angle into ¼-inch-thick slices. Cut 1 slice of bread lengthwise in half and then crosswise into thirds, to make 6 pieces. Place a slice of banana on each piece of bread. Stack 4 pieces of the banana-topped bread, turn the stack on its side, and place it in a ramekin. Put the 2 remaining pieces of bread, banana side inward, on either side of the stack. Repeat to fill the remaining ramekins.

TO MAKE THE CUSTARD Whisk the eggs, 1 tablespoon of the sugar, the salt, and vanilla in a medium bowl just until blended but not foamy. Whisk in the half-and-half and milk. Fill each ramekin with the egg mixture, reserving any left over. Let stand until the bread is saturated, 20 to 30 minutes, topping off the puddings with the remaining egg mixture as necessary.

Position a rack in the lower third of the oven and preheat the oven to 400°F. Put a kettle of water on to boil. Brush or drizzle the exposed edges of the bread with the melted butter, then sprinkle the buttered edges with the remaining tablespoon of sugar, using a generous ¼ teaspoon per pudding.

Wipe any smudges off the ramekins and set them in the baking pan. Put the pan in the oven. Pull out the oven rack and pour boiling water into the pan to come halfway up the sides of the ramekins. Bake for 20 to 30 minutes, until the edges of the bread are golden brown and a knife inserted in the puddings comes out mostly clean. Let cool for 10 minutes in the water bath, then remove with tongs. If not serving within 2 hours, cover and refrigerate.

Serve the puddings in their cups, warm, at room temperature, or cold, or reheated individually for a few seconds in the microwave. Or unmold them: slide a thin knife around the inside of each ramekin to detach the pudding, tip the ramekin on a dessert dish, and slide the pudding out, letting the sauce flow around it. Scrape the extra sauce from the cup around it or drizzle on top.

BLACK-AND-WHITE BREAD PUDDING

You can't have too many good bread pudding recipes. This one features a brownie-like mixture slathered on the slices of bread, which are then drenched in custard. The contrast is superb.

Serves 6 to 8

INGREDIENTS

FOR THE FILLING

4 tablespoons (2 ounces) unsalted butter

2 ounces unsweetened chocolate, chopped

½ cup (3.5 ounces) sugar

⅛ teaspoon salt

1 cold large egg

1 tablespoon unbleached all-purpose flour

7 thin slices slightly stale or very lightly toasted firm white sandwich bread (such as Pepperidge Farm or Oroweat/Arnold's Country Buttermilk or Country Potato Bread) or enough slices of baguette or challah to fill the baking dish with 2½ layers

FOR THE CUSTARD

4 large eggs

½ cup (3.5 ounces) sugar

Pinch of salt

1¼ teaspoons pure vanilla extract

3 cups whole milk

1 tablespoon unsalted butter, melted

EQUIPMENT

8-inch square baking dish

Medium-fine-mesh strainer

Baking pan large enough to hold the baking dish with space all around it

✳ **VARIATION**

Nutella Bread Pudding

Substitute about ⅓ cup Nutella for the chocolate filling. It's quicker and easier . . . and sooo good!

121

DIRECTIONS

TO MAKE THE FILLING Heat the butter in a small saucepan until it is melted and beginning to simmer. Off the heat, whisk in the chocolate until it is melted. Scrape the mixture into a medium bowl. Whisk in the sugar and salt, then whisk in the egg. Add the flour and whisk briskly until the mixture is thick and smooth. Refrigerate for at least 15 minutes (or up to 2 days).

Spread the chocolate filling evenly over one side of each bread slice. Cut large slices (not baguette slices) into quarters. Arrange the bread slices chocolate side up in one crowded overlapping layer in the baking dish (the pieces will almost be standing on end).

TO MAKE THE CUSTARD Whisk the eggs, sugar, salt, and vanilla in a medium bowl just until blended but not foamy. Stir in the milk. Strain the mixture over the bread. Cover the pudding with plastic wrap. Put another baking dish on top to submerge the bread. Let stand for 20 minutes, or until the bread has absorbed the liquid.

Position a rack in the lower third of the oven and preheat the oven to 325°F. Put a kettle of water on to boil.

Uncover the pudding. Brush or drizzle the melted butter onto the exposed edges of the bread. Put the dish in the larger baking pan, set the pan in the oven, and pull out the rack. Pour boiling water into the larger pan to come halfway up the sides of the baking dish. Bake for 45 to 50 minutes, until a knife inserted in the pudding comes out free of custard (ignore any chocolate that may be clinging to it). Remove the baking dish from the water bath and let cool. If not serving within 2 hours, cover and refrigerate.

Serve warm or at room temperature. Cold leftover pudding is divine, but you can also reheat it in the microwave on medium power for a few seconds.

SOUR CREAM SOUFFLÉS

Serve these effortlessly simple, lovely golden soufflés plain or accessorize them with fruit or fruit sauces, such as Saucy Berries (page 81), Honey Balsamic Sauce (page 16), Maple Cranberry Sauce (page 80), or Dessert Chutney (page 82). Or you can lace them with chopped chocolate (see the photograph on page 125 and the variations on page 124). Instead of sour cream, you can use ricotta, Greek yogurt, or mascarpone; each has its differences, and each is delicious.

Serves 6

INGREDIENTS

Softened unsalted butter and sugar for coating the ramekins

One 8-ounce container sour cream

3 large eggs, separated

3 tablespoons unbleached all-purpose flour

⅛ teaspoon salt

1 teaspoon pure vanilla extract

1 teaspoon finely grated lemon, orange, or tangerine zest

⅛ teaspoon cream of tartar

5 tablespoons sugar, plus more for sprinkling

EQUIPMENT

Six 6-ounce ramekins

Baking sheet

Electric mixer

DIRECTIONS

Position a rack in the center of the oven and preheat the oven to 375°F. Butter and sugar the ramekins and place them on the baking sheet.

Continued

Continued

✳ **TIP**

Make the soufflés ahead and bake just before serving.

✳ **GOOD TO KNOW**

The Best Way to Sugar Cups

Butter all the ramekins first, then add a couple tablespoons of sugar to one and shake and rotate it until coated. Pour the excess sugar into the next cup and repeat.

Combine the sour cream, egg yolks, flour, salt, vanilla, and citrus zest in a large bowl and stir until blended.

With the electric mixer, beat the egg whites with the cream of tartar in another large clean, dry bowl at medium speed until soft peaks form when the beaters are lifted. Gradually add the sugar, continuing to beat at high speed until the whites are stiff but not dry.

Fold about one-quarter of the egg whites into the sour cream mixture, then fold in the remaining egg whites.

Divide the batter among the ramekins, filling them nearly full. (The unbaked soufflés can be covered and refrigerated for up to 24 hours.)

Sprinkle the top of each soufflé with sugar. Bake the soufflés for 15 to 18 minutes (or a couple of minutes longer if the soufflés have been chilled), until they are puffed and slightly golden brown. Serve immediately, with sauce, if desired.

✳ VARIATIONS

Chocolate-Laced Sour Cream Soufflés

Omit the citrus zest. Fold ¼ cup chopped bittersweet or semisweet chocolate into the batter with the egg whites. Sprinkle the tops with a little extra chocolate. Increase the baking time by a couple of minutes.

Sour Cream Soufflés with Berries on the Bottom

After buttering and sugaring the ramekins, drop 5 or 6 raspberries, or 4 or 5 blackberries or boysenberries, into each one; they should fit loosely, with space between them. Sprinkle a generous ½ teaspoon sugar over the berries in each ramekin. Proceed as directed.

BITTERSWEET COCOA SOUFFLÉS

These terrifically simple cocoa soufflés are loaded with shards of melty, gooey bittersweet chocolate. They can be prepared in advance—all except for the baking. Just before serving time, slide them into a preheated oven while you clear the table for coffee.

Serves 8

INGREDIENTS

Softened unsalted butter and sugar for coating the ramekins

½ cup plus 3 tablespoons (4.8 ounces) sugar

2 tablespoons unbleached all-purpose flour

Scant ⅛ teaspoon salt

⅔ cup whole milk

½ cup (1.625 ounces) unsweetened cocoa powder, preferably natural

3 tablespoons water

2 large eggs, separated, plus 2 large egg whites

1 teaspoon pure vanilla extract

⅛ teaspoon cream of tartar

3 ounces semisweet or bittersweet chocolate (any cacao percentage), finely chopped, or ½ cup chocolate chips

Powdered sugar (optional)

Lightly Sweetened Whipped Cream (page 130) or Coffee Whipped Cream (page 131)

EQUIPMENT

Eight 5- to 6-ounce ramekins

Baking sheet

Electric mixer

✳ **VARIATION**

Bittersweet Cocoa Soufflés with Orange Blossom Cream

Serve the soufflés with Orange Blossom Whipped Cream (page 131) and grate a little cinnamon stick over each before serving.

DIRECTIONS

Position a rack in the lower third of the oven and preheat the oven to 375°F. Butter the ramekins lightly but thoroughly and sprinkle them with sugar, coating them completely, and place on the baking sheet.

Whisk ½ cup of the sugar with the flour and salt in a small saucepan. Whisk a little of the milk into the sugar mixture to form a thick paste. Gradually whisk in the remaining milk. Cook over medium-low heat, stirring with a silicone spatula or a wooden spoon, until bubbles appear around the edges of the pan, then continue cooking, stirring constantly to prevent scorching, until the mixture is slightly thickened, about 2 minutes longer. Scrape the mixture into a large bowl. Stir in the cocoa powder, water, egg yolks, and vanilla to form a thick, smooth paste. Set aside.

With the electric mixer, beat the egg whites with the cream of tartar in another large clean, dry bowl at medium speed until soft peaks form when the beaters are lifted. Gradually add the remaining 3 tablespoons sugar, continuing to beat at high speed until the egg whites are stiff but not dry.

Fold about one-quarter of the egg whites into the cocoa mixture to lighten it. Add the remaining egg whites and the chopped chocolate and fold in until blended.

Divide the batter among the ramekins, filling them nearly full. (The unbaked soufflés can be covered and refrigerated for up to a day ahead.)

Bake the soufflés for about 12 minutes (15 minutes if they've been chilled), until they puff up (they may crack on top) and a toothpick inserted in the center comes out with just a little thickened batter clinging to it. Sieve a little powdered sugar over the soufflés, if desired.

Serve immediately. Pass the bowl of whipped cream separately for guests to serve themselves or use a spoon to break the surface of each soufflé and top with a dollop of whipped cream.

WHIPPED CREAM

Whipped cream may be the easiest and best choice you can make for topping or filling many desserts. Unlike with frosting or buttercream, you can leave it unsweetened or sweeten it as much as you like. Unlike custard, it is neutral in flavor. Whipped cream accentuates the flavor of anything you put it on by providing contrast; it adds creamy richness to light tangy ingredients like fruit, and intensifies the flavor of dark chocolate. And nothing could be simpler to make!

5 RULES FOR WHIPPED CREAM

1] Use heavy whipping cream. The best and freshest-tasting cream is not ultra-pasteurized, sterilized, or stabilized with starch or carrageenan. If you have the choice, look for an ingredient list with nothing on it but cream.

2] Cream should be very cold when you whip it. If you've just come from the store, refrigerate the cream for a while before you whip it. Cream that isn't cold enough will either refuse to thicken or eventually curdle when you whip it. For extra whipped cream insurance, chill the bowl and the beaters in the freezer before whipping the cream!

3] You can sweeten whipped cream with either granulated sugar (my preference, because it has no starch in it) or powdered sugar (which contains a little cornstarch). When the cream starts to thicken, gradually add the sugar, then taste and adjust the sweetness toward the end of beating: cream tastes less sweet when it's fluffy than when it's fluid. Vanilla adds flavor and a nuance of sweetness too; add ½ to 1 teaspoon pure vanilla extract per cup of cream when you start beating.

4] You can whip cream so that it is just thickened enough to flow like a sauce or stiff enough to hold a crisp shape. But don't whip it until very stiff or it will be grainy on the palate (from the specks of butter that will form). You can whip cream in advance and refrigerate it until needed. Just before using, fold it or give it a few strokes of the whisk to reincorporate any cream that may have settled at the bottom of the bowl.

5] If you plan to pipe whipped cream with a pastry bag, spread it over a cake for filling or frosting, or fold it into another mixture, always whip it to less stiff than you want it to be. Piping, spreading, or folding will all stiffen the cream, and if it is stiff to begin with, it will be over-whipped and granular by the time you are finished.

LIGHTLY SWEETENED WHIPPED CREAM

Makes 2 to 2½ cups

INGREDIENTS

1 cup heavy cream

½ teaspoon pure vanilla extract (optional)

2 to 3 teaspoons sugar, or more to taste

DIRECTIONS

Using chilled beaters (or a whisk), beat the cream with the vanilla, if using, in a chilled bowl until it holds a soft shape. Gradually add the sugar and beat until it holds a good shape but is not too stiff. (See 5 Rules for Whipped Cream, page 129.)

✳ VARIATIONS

Unsweetened Whipped Cream

Omit the sugar.

Lightly Sweetened Crème Fraîche

Substitute crème fraîche for all or any amount of the heavy cream.

✳ GOOD TO KNOW

You can lighten whipped cream by adding ¼ cup Greek yogurt or sour cream to it before whipping.

10 WAYS TO FLAVOR WHIPPED CREAM

As much as I adore plain whipped cream, I also love that it can be flavored. It loses its marvelous neutral character and becomes a flavor component in its own right, and sometimes that is exactly what you want.

1] COFFEE WHIPPED CREAM

Stir 2 teaspoons espresso powder or 2½ teaspoons freeze-dried coffee crystals and a generous tablespoon of sugar into 1 cup heavy cream. Whip as usual, tasting and adjusting the sweetness toward the end.

Tastes good with: chocolate desserts, strawberries, pineapple.

2] COCOA WHIPPED CREAM

Use 1 tablespoon unsweetened cocoa powder and 4 teaspoons sugar for 1 cup heavy cream. Mix the cocoa and sugar with a tablespoon or two of the cream to form a thick paste (this serves to eliminate lumps in the cocoa) before stirring in the rest of the cream. (For Mocha Whipped Cream, add 1½ to 2 teaspoons espresso powder or freeze-dried coffee crystals to taste.) For the thickest texture and richest flavor, refrigerate for an hour or overnight before whipping.

Tastes good with: chocolate desserts.

3] NIBBY WHIPPED CREAM

Start at least several hours ahead. Combine 1 cup heavy cream and 2 tablespoons roasted cacao nibs in a saucepan and bring to a simmer. Turn off the heat, cover the pan, and let steep for 20 minutes. Strain the cream into a bowl, pressing on the nibs to extract as much liquid as possible; discard the nibs. Refrigerate the cream for at least several hours, or overnight, before whipping, adding sugar to taste.

Tastes good with: chocolate desserts, meringues and pavlova (see pages 160 and 161), coffee drinks, sweetened blackberries.

4] JASMINE WHIPPED CREAM

Start at least 8 hours ahead. Stir 1 tablespoon good-quality jasmine tea leaves into 1 cup heavy cream. Cover and refrigerate for 8 to 12 hours (no longer).

Strain the cream into a bowl, pressing on the tea leaves to extract as much liquid as possible; discard the tea leaves. Whip the cream with 2 teaspoons sugar; or refrigerate it to whip up to a day later.

Tastes good with: rich chocolate desserts.

5] ORANGE BLOSSOM WHIPPED CREAM

Add 1½ teaspoons sugar, 1 teaspoon finely grated orange zest, and ¾ teaspoon orange flower water to 1 cup heavy cream. Whip as usual, tasting and adjusting the flavor and sweetness toward the end.

Tastes good with: chocolate desserts.

6] ROSE WHIPPED CREAM

Add 1½ teaspoons sugar and ½ teaspoon rose water to 1 cup heavy cream. Whip as usual, tasting and adjusting the flavor and sweetness toward the end.

Continued

Tastes good with: berries (in particular, strawberries), watermelon, chocolate desserts.

7] HALVAH WHIPPED CREAM

Use ¼ cup or more finely grated or crumbled halvah and 1 tablespoon of sugar (or more to taste) for 1 cup of cream. Whip and sweeten the cream as usual, then fold in the halvah. Or whip the halvah with the cream to start with, adding sugar to taste along the way; it won't get as fluffy, but the flavor will be more pronounced and the texture smoother.

Tastes good with: strawberries.

8] LEMON WHIPPED CREAM

Use 1 tablespoon sugar and 2½ to 3 tablespoons cold Lemon Curd (page 231) for 1 cup heavy cream. Whip the cream with the sugar until fairly thick but not quite stiff. Whisk in the lemon curd.

Tastes good with: strawberries or blueberries, Fresh Ginger Gingerbread (page 213).

9] FRESH MINT WHIPPED CREAM

Start at least 8 hours ahead. Stir ¼ cup coarsely chopped fresh mint leaves into 1 cup heavy cream. Cover and refrigerate for 8 to 12 hours (no longer). Strain the cream into a bowl, pressing on the mint leaves to extract as much liquid as possible; discard the mint. Whip the cream with sugar to taste; or refrigerate it to whip up to a day later.

Tastes good with: strawberries or other berries, bananas, sponge cake, chocolate desserts, coffee drinks.

10] PRALINE WHIPPED CREAM

Use ½ cup to 1¼ cups (to taste) finely chopped or crushed Praline (page 32) for 1 cup heavy cream. Whip the cream until it holds a soft shape. If you fold in the crushed praline shortly before serving, it will retain its lovely crunch. If you whip the cream and add the praline a few hours in advance, the cream will dissolve the caramelized sugar and take on more of the burnt sugar flavor and color, though the bits of praline will be less crunchy. Divine either way!

Tastes good with: Berries, peaches, nectarines, bananas, apricots, chocolate desserts. Or use to top or fill a simple sponge cake or a nutty sponge cake. It's a superb filling for cream puffs too.

CHOCOLATE WHIPPED CREAM 3 WAYS

Sometimes a dessert needs a topping that is richer than plain whipped cream, but lighter and less intense than ganache. Start at least 4 hours, or up to a day, ahead to allow the cream to chill before you whip it.

DARK CHOCOLATE WHIPPED CREAM

Makes about 1½ cups

3 ounces semisweet or bittersweet chocolate (not more than 62% cacao), chopped medium-fine

1 cup heavy cream

A pinch or two of salt (optional)

Put the chocolate in a medium bowl. Bring the cream to a gentle boil in a large heavy saucepan and pour over the chocolate. Let stand for 30 seconds, then stir well. Let stand for 15 minutes or so to finish melting every last speck of chocolate, then stir until the mixture looks perfectly uniform. Let cool. Taste and add salt, if desired. Cover and refrigerate for at least 4 hours, or until completely chilled (I like to leave it overnight, and it can be prepared to this point up to 4 days ahead).

To serve, whip the cream with an electric mixer until it lightens and holds a shape (it won't be smooth if you overwhip it). Use immediately or refrigerate until needed.

MILK CHOCOLATE WHIPPED CREAM

Hard to believe, but adding a little water to this mixture sharpens the flavor of the chocolate!

Makes about 2 cups

4 ounces milk chocolate, finely chopped

¾ cup heavy cream

3 tablespoons water

A pinch or two of salt (optional)

Put the chocolate in a medium bowl. Bring the cream and water to a simmer in a saucepan and pour over the chocolate. Let stand for 30 seconds, then stir well. Let stand for 15 minutes or so to finish melting the chocolate, then stir again until every last bit of the chocolate is melted into the cream. Let cool. Taste and add salt, if desired. Cover and refrigerate for at least several hours, or until completely chilled (I like to leave it overnight, and it can be prepared to this point up to 4 days ahead).

To serve, whip the cream with an electric mixer until it holds a shape (it won't be smooth if you overwhip it). Use immediately or refrigerate until needed.

WHITE CHOCOLATE WHIPPED CREAM

Makes about 2 cups

4 ounces white chocolate, finely chopped

¾ cup heavy cream

3 tablespoons water

A pinch or two of salt (optional)

Put the chocolate in a medium bowl. Bring the cream and water to a simmer in a saucepan and pour over the chocolate. Let stand for 30 seconds, then stir well. Let stand for 15 minutes or so to finish melting the chocolate, then stir again until every last bit of chocolate is melted into the cream. Let cool. Taste and add salt, if desired. Cover and refrigerate for at least several hours, or until completely chilled (I like to leave it overnight, and it can be prepared to this point up to 4 days ahead).

To serve, whip the cream with an electric mixer until it holds a shape (it won't be smooth if you overwhip it). Use immediately or refrigerate until needed.

QUICK PIES, TARTS, AND MERINGUES

These most fabulous pies and tarts take very little time, with very little fuss. I've eliminated all of the classic pastry doughs and even the rolling pin in this short, sweet collection of great-looking, elegant desserts, perfect for company (with many do-ahead steps). With the traditional pastry and rolling pin go the worry and the mess on the counter. Instead, I give you quick and tasty crumb crusts for pudding pies and melted butter press-in dough for tarts. And along with them, you get my favorite meringue desserts, from a crunchy melt-in-your-mouth almond butter meringue to a classic pavlova (with not-so-classic variations), crusty crunchy on the outside and marshmallowy sweet within.

PASTRY PANIC

Even accomplished cooks suffer from pastry panic: Will it be flaky or tough? Will it crack when I roll it, will it stick to the counter, will it break when I lift it? And what the heck do they mean when they say, "Don't overwork the dough"? I am going to help you avoid all of the potentially scary issues by simply eliminating them: I've chosen pies and tarts with two easy and forgiving crusts that happen to be superb. They are impossible to overwork, and you won't be asked to roll them or lift them!

1] **PRESS-IN CRUMB CRUSTS** Made with graham crackers or purchased chocolate wafers, these crusts are gold. With either version, you get a fast, flavorful, sweet, and crunchy counterpoint under a silky pudding filling. And these crusts are sog proof because they are coated with a little slick of chocolate (melted right on the hot crust—no need to dirty another bowl).

Most recipes for crumb crusts use more butter than mine do to make sure the crumbs are completely coated. I use less butter, mix the ingredients thoroughly, and press the crumbs firmly into the pan with the flat bottom of a glass or a cup. Less butter makes the crust less likely to slide down the sides of the pie pan while baking and also produces a crunchier, more delicious crust. So use a level crumb measurement, mix thoroughly, and press firmly. That's all.

2] **PRESS-IN SWEET CRUST (AKA SHORT-BREAD OR COOKIE CRUST)** This recipe (and

variation) is my treasure. It is the most delicious sweet crust I know, and as forgiving as Play-Doh to work with. It's made with melted butter, so no worries about whether the butter is too soft or too firm. When the crust is fully baked—and don't be fainthearted about getting it deeply golden brown—it is divinely crunchy and tender. Always. In addition, it barely shrinks in the oven, so you don't need to fool with messy pie weights.

After mixing, the dough may seem too soft and greasy. Don't worry, just proceed. Or you can let it stand for 5 minutes at room temperature; it will firm up as the butter cools. There is just enough dough, not too much or too little—you will use all of it to line one 9½-inch tart pan. Don't worry about overworking: just press the dough as evenly as you can over the bottom of the pan and up the sides. Use the heel of your hand to flatten the bottom of the crust, or smooth it with the bottom of a glass, or with a scraper or a spatula. It may seem at first that there is not enough

dough, but trust me, there is. Press the side of your finger or the bottom of a glass into the corners of the pan—extra dough usually hides there—and then press it up the sides of the pan; or pinch some off from a thicker area and press it in wherever you need it. The dough on the sides of the pan should be evenly thick and squared off at the top (rather than tapered) to prevent the crust from shrinking down or the top edge from burning. So take an extra minute or so if necessary when lining the pan. You will be rewarded with an evenly baked, beautiful, delicious crust.

One more tip: when baking an unfilled tart crust (as for Sour Cream and Brown Sugar Tart, page 147), always bake the crust until it's fully golden brown all over, even if it will be put back into the oven after it is filled to bake the filling. Partially baked crusts that are filled and put back into the oven will not finish baking with the filling—your dessert will end up with an underbaked, pasty, soggy crust.

MILK CHOCOLATE PUDDING PIE
WITH SALTED PEANUT CRUST

Rich, sweet, smooth milk chocolate pudding in a crunchy crust with a touch of salt, topped with slightly tangy whipped cream and salted peanuts. (Photograph on page 134)

Serves 8 to 10

INGREDIENTS

FOR THE CRUST

¼ cup (1 ounce) salted roasted peanuts (finely ground in a food processor or crushed in a bag with a rolling pin)

2 tablespoons sugar

¾ cup (2.5 ounces) graham cracker crumbs (finely ground in a food processor)

4 tablespoons (2 ounces) unsalted butter, melted

3 ounces milk chocolate, finely chopped

FOR THE FILLING

3 tablespoons sugar

3 tablespoons unsweetened cocoa powder, preferably natural

2 tablespoons plus 2 teaspoons cornstarch

⅛ teaspoon salt

2 cups whole milk

7 ounces milk chocolate, very finely chopped

1½ recipes Unsweetened Whipped Cream (page 130)

A couple of tablespoons of salted roasted peanuts

EQUIPMENT

Food processor

9-inch pie plate

✻ GOOD TO KNOW

You can substitute the ingredients for any of the Cookie Crunch recipes on page 30 for this crust, or you can substitute the crust for Chocolate Pudding Pie on page 139.

DIRECTIONS

Position a rack in the lower third of the oven and preheat the oven to 350°F.

TO MAKE THE CRUST Mix the peanuts, sugar, graham cracker crumbs, and butter in a medium bowl until the mixture is evenly moistened. Spread the mixture in the pie plate and use the bottom of a glass or a custard cup to press it evenly and firmly over the bottom and up the sides of the pie plate.

Bake for 12 to 14 minutes, until the crust begins to set and colors slightly. If the crust puffs up while baking, press it gently back into place with the back of a fork or the custard cup.

Remove the crust from the oven, sprinkle the chopped chocolate over the bottom, and let the chocolate soften for 1 to 2 minutes. Using a pastry brush or the back of a spoon, spread the chocolate evenly over the bottom and up the sides of the crust. Let cool, then chill the crust until the chocolate sets, about 30 minutes.

TO MAKE THE FILLING Whisk the sugar, cocoa, cornstarch, and salt together in a heavy medium saucepan. Add about 3 tablespoons of the milk and whisk to form a smooth paste. Whisk in the remaining milk. Using a silicone spatula or a wooden spoon, stir the mixture constantly over medium heat, scraping the bottom, sides, and corners of the pan, until the pudding thickens and begins to bubble at the edges, about 5 minutes. Continue to cook and stir for 1 minute, then add the chocolate and stir briskly until the chocolate is melted and the pudding is smooth, about 30 seconds longer. Scrape the hot pudding into the crust and level it with one or two strokes of the spatula. Let cool for 1 hour, then refrigerate the pie. When the filling is cool, cover and chill for at least several hours, or overnight.

Top the pie with dollops or a swirl of the whipped cream, and sprinkle with the peanuts.

CHOCOLATE PUDDING PIE

A classic chocolate pudding pie, dialed up with more dark chocolate and less sugar and corn-starch in the filling. A topping of whipped cream is never out of style, but whipped crème fraîche—or a combination of the two—adds an exciting edge.

Serves 8 to 10

INGREDIENTS

FOR THE CRUST

1 cup (4.5 ounces) chocolate cookie crumbs (about half of a 9-ounce package of chocolate wafers, finely ground in a food processor or crushed in a bag with a rolling pin)

2 tablespoons sugar

4 tablespoons (2 ounces) unsalted butter, melted

2 ounces bittersweet or semisweet chocolate (any cacao percentage), finely chopped

FOR THE FILLING

⅓ cup (2.33 ounces) sugar

⅓ cup (1 ounce) unsweetened cocoa powder, preferably natural

2 tablespoons cornstarch

⅛ teaspoon salt

1¾ cups whole milk

¼ cup heavy cream

3 to 4 ounces bittersweet or semisweet chocolate (use the lesser amount for chocolate in the 70% cacao range and the full 4 ounces for one closer to 60%), finely chopped

1 teaspoon pure vanilla extract

1 tablespoon dark rum (optional)

1½ recipes Lightly Sweetened Whipped Cream (page 130) or Lightly Sweetened Crème Fraîche (page 130)

Chocolate shavings, Totally Doable Chocolate Shards (page 232), or unsweetened cocoa powder for garnish

✳ GOOD TO KNOW

You can play around with this pie. Fill it with the milk chocolate filling from the pie on page 137, or make the variation with a spicy crust and garnish on page 140.

EQUIPMENT

Food processor (optional)

9-inch pie plate

DIRECTIONS

Position a rack in the lower third of the oven and preheat the oven to 350°F.

TO MAKE THE CRUST Mix the cookie crumbs with the sugar and butter in a medium bowl until the crumbs are moistened. Spread the mixture in the pie plate and use the bottom of a glass to press it evenly and firmly over the bottom and up the sides of the pie plate. Bake for 12 to 14 minutes, until the crust begins to set and no longer looks moist. If the crust puffs up while baking, press it gently back into place with the back of a fork or the custard cup.

Remove the crust from the oven, sprinkle the chopped chocolate over the bottom, and let the chocolate soften for 1 to 2 minutes. Using a pastry brush or the back of a spoon, spread the chocolate evenly over the bottom and up the sides of the crust. Let cool, then chill the crust until the chocolate sets, about 30 minutes.

TO MAKE THE FILLING Whisk the sugar, cocoa, cornstarch, and salt together in a heavy medium saucepan. Add about 3 tablespoons of the milk and whisk to form a smooth paste. Whisk in the remaining milk and the cream. Using a silicone spatula or a wooden spoon, stir the mixture constantly over medium heat until the pudding thickens and begins to bubble at the edges, about 5 minutes. Continue to cook and stir for 1 minute, then add the chocolate and stir briskly until the chocolate is melted and the pudding is smooth, about 30 seconds longer. Remove from the heat and stir in the vanilla and rum, if using. Scrape the hot pudding into the crust and level it with one or two strokes of the spatula. Let cool for 1 hour, then refrigerate the pie. When the filling is cool, cover and chill for at least several hours, or overnight.

Top the pie with the whipped cream. Garnish with chocolate shavings or shards, or a dusting of cocoa powder.

✳ VARIATION

Chocolate Pudding Pie with Ancho Chile and Cinnamon

For the crust, substitute 1 cup graham cracker crumbs and ⅓ cup ground pecans for the chocolate cookie crumbs. Increase the sugar to 3 tablespoons and add ¼ teaspoon salt, ½ teaspoon ground cinnamon, and ½ teaspoon ground ancho chile. Substitute 3 ounces milk chocolate for the 2 ounces dark chocolate in the crust.

Make and chill the pie as directed. Finish the pie with the whipped cream. Sprinkle the cream with pinches of ground ancho chile, grated cinnamon stick, and shaved or grated milk chocolate.

BITTERSWEET CHOCOLATE TART

This gooey, bittersweet "brownie" baked on a melt-in-your-mouth shortbread crust studded with walnuts and topped with whipped cream or whipped crème fraîche is decadent and sexy.

Serves 10

INGREDIENTS

FOR THE FILLING

8 ounces bittersweet chocolate (70% cacao), coarsely chopped

6 tablespoons (3 ounces) unsalted butter, cut into chunks

2 large eggs

1 cup (7 ounces) sugar

1 teaspoon pure vanilla extract

¼ teaspoon salt

¼ cup (1.125 ounces) unbleached all-purpose flour

FOR THE CRUST

8 tablespoons (4 ounces) unsalted butter, melted

¼ cup (1.75 ounces) sugar

¼ teaspoon salt

¼ teaspoon pure vanilla extract

1 cup plus 2 tablespoons (5 ounces) unbleached all-purpose flour

⅔ cup (2.3 ounces) walnuts, coarsely chopped

Unsweetened Whipped Cream (page 130) or whipped crème fraîche

A whole nutmeg or cinnamon stick (optional)

EQUIPMENT

Electric mixer

9½-inch fluted tart pan with a removable bottom

Baking sheet

✳ GOOD TO KNOW

This tart is especially seductive served warm and with the optional grating of spice. You can pass the whole nutmeg or cinnamon stick with the grater and let guests choose and grate their own. Everyone will leave with fragrant fingers.

DIRECTIONS

Position a rack in the lower third of the oven and preheat the oven to 350°F.

TO MAKE THE FILLING Put the chocolate and butter in a medium heatproof bowl, preferably stainless steel, set it in a wide skillet of barely simmering water (see Melting Chocolate My Way, page 97), and stir frequently until the chocolate and butter are melted, smooth, and very warm to the touch. Remove the bowl from the skillet and set aside.

With the electric mixer, beat the eggs, sugar, vanilla, and salt in a medium bowl at high speed until the mixture is thick and light in color, 3 to 4 minutes. Scrape the warm chocolate mixture into the bowl and fold in with a rubber spatula. Fold in the flour. Set aside.

TO MAKE THE CRUST Combine the melted butter with the sugar, salt, and vanilla in a bowl. Stir in the flour and mix just until blended. If the dough seems too soft and gooey, let it stand for a few minutes to firm up. Press the dough evenly over the bottom and up the sides of the tart pan to make a very thin even layer. There is just enough dough; press the dough squarely into the corners of the pan to avoid ending up with extra-thick edges. Scatter the nuts evenly over the dough in the bottom of the pan and press them into the dough as far as they will go.

Put the pan on the baking sheet. Bake for 20 to 25 minutes, until the crust is fully golden brown all over. Remove the pan from the oven, leaving the oven on.

Scrape the chocolate filling onto the hot crust and spread it evenly with a spatula. Return to the oven and bake for 20 to 22 minutes, just until a toothpick inserted in two or three places comes out clean or with only a stray crumb. Set the pan on a rack to cool.

Remove the sides of the tart pan and transfer the tart to a serving platter. Serve each slice with a dollop of the whipped cream, offering a grating of nutmeg or cinnamon on top, if desired. The tart keeps at room temperature, covered, for 2 to 3 days.

TAHITIAN VANILLA TART
WITH WINTER CHERRY COMPOTE

Tahitian vanilla has an exotic flavor and nuances of cherry, lovely in this cozy vanilla pudding tart with a cherry compote. When I tasted the crust separately, I thought at first the nutmeg was a mistake, but the ensemble, with pudding and cherries, turned out to be extra good.

Serves 8

INGREDIENTS

FOR THE CRUST

8 tablespoons (4 ounces) unsalted butter, melted

¼ cup (1.75 ounces) sugar

¾ teaspoon pure Tahitian vanilla extract

⅛ teaspoon ground nutmeg

¼ teaspoon salt

1 cup plus 2 tablespoons (5 ounces) unbleached all-purpose flour

FOR THE FILLING

¼ cup (1.75 ounces) sugar

2 tablespoons plus 2 teaspoons cornstarch

⅛ teaspoon salt

2 cups half-and-half

2 teaspoons pure Tahitian vanilla extract

Winter Cherry Compote (page 146)

EQUIPMENT

9½-inch fluted tart pan with a removable bottom

Baking sheet

✳ TIP

You can substitute pure Bourbon or Mexican vanilla extract for the Tahitian vanilla, of course! Or you can heat the milk and cream with a whole vanilla bean until steaming hot, then cover and let steep for 15 minutes. Fish out the bean and set it aside. Proceed with the recipe. Rinse and dry the vanilla bean and put it away for another use.

DIRECTIONS

Position a rack in the lower third of the oven and preheat the oven to 350°F.

TO MAKE THE CRUST Combine the butter, sugar, vanilla, nutmeg, and salt in a medium bowl. Add the flour and mix just until well blended. If the dough seems too soft and gooey, let it stand for a few minutes to firm up.

Press the dough evenly over the bottom and up the sides of the tart pan to make a thin, even layer. This takes a bit of patience, as there is just enough dough. Press the dough squarely into the corners of the pan to avoid extra-thick edges. (The crust can be prepared 2 to 3 days ahead to this point, wrapped, and refrigerated; bring to room temperature before baking.)

Put the pan on the baking sheet. Bake for 20 to 25 minutes, until the crust is fully golden brown all over. If the crust puffs up during baking, gently press it down with the back of a fork and prick it a few times. Cool the crust on a rack.

TO MAKE THE FILLING Whisk the sugar, cornstarch, and salt together in a heavy medium saucepan. Add about 3 tablespoons of the half-and-half and whisk to form a smooth paste. Whisk in the remaining half-and-half. Using a silicone spatula or a wooden spoon, stir the mixture constantly over medium heat, scraping the bottom, sides, and corners of the pan, until the pudding thickens and begins to bubble at the edges, about 5 minutes. Continue to cook and stir for 1 more minute. Remove from the heat and stir in the vanilla extract.

Scrape the hot pudding into the crust and level it with one or two strokes of the spatula. Let cool for 1 hour, then refrigerate the tart for at least 2 hours before serving. (Cover the tart once the filling is set.)

Serve the tart with the cherry compote.

WINTER CHERRY COMPOTE

Vanilla bean pulls out some interesting earthy, woody flavor notes from the wine, and vice versa. The longer you keep the compote, the tastier it gets. Make it ahead or keep it on hand to spoon over ice cream.

Makes about 1 cup

INGREDIENTS

2 cups dry red wine, such as Merlot

2 tablespoons sugar, or to taste

½ vanilla bean, split

½ cup dried sour or sweet (Bing) cherries, or a combination (I like the sour ones)

DIRECTIONS

Combine the wine, sugar, and vanilla bean in a small saucepan, bring to a simmer, and simmer until the wine reduces to about ¾ cup.

Add the cherries, cover the pan, and simmer for a few minutes to plump them. Taste and add sugar if the mixture seems too tart. Remove from the heat and let cool, then cover and refrigerate until needed. Leave the vanilla bean in the compote until ready to serve. Rinse and dry the vanilla bean and put it away for a later use. The compote keeps for at least 2 weeks in a covered container in the refrigerator.

✳ GOOD TO KNOW

Make the compote days ahead; it just gets better. In summer you can add a handful of pitted fresh cherries along with the dried cherries.

SOUR CREAM AND BROWN SUGAR TART

This delicate sour cream custard turns a pale golden ivory in the oven. The contrast of the cultured cream and the sweet brown-sugar toffee-flavored crust is perfection. Add a little spoonful of fresh berries on the side if you must garnish this gem. If you enjoy dessert wines, try a Canadian ice wine. Bake the tart on the day you will serve it.

Serves 8

INGREDIENTS

FOR THE CRUST

8 tablespoons (4 ounces) unsalted butter, melted

¼ cup (1.75 ounces) firmly packed brown sugar

¼ teaspoon salt

¾ teaspoon pure vanilla extract

1 cup plus 2 tablespoons (5 ounces) unbleached all-purpose flour

FOR THE FILLING

3 large eggs

¼ cup (1.75 ounces) sugar

⅛ teaspoon salt

½ teaspoon pure vanilla extract

1¼ cups sour cream

1 large egg yolk, beaten with a pinch of salt

A carton of strawberries, rinsed, hulled, and quartered, or ½ pint raspberries or ripe (not too tart) blackberries (optional)

EQUIPMENT

9½-inch fluted tart pan with a removable bottom

Baking sheet

✳ GOOD TO KNOW

If berries are sweet and ripe, nothing needs to be done to them. Alternatively, they can be tossed with fresh lemon juice, a sprinkling of sugar, and a grating of zest to taste. This treatment will help brighten less-than-perfect berries.

DIRECTIONS

Position a rack in the lower third of the oven and preheat the oven to 350°F.

TO MAKE THE CRUST Combine the butter, brown sugar, salt, and vanilla in a medium bowl. Add the flour and mix just until well blended. If the dough seems too soft and gooey, let it stand for a few minutes to firm up.

Press the dough evenly over the bottom and up the sides of the tart pan to make a thin, even layer. This takes a bit of patience, as there is just enough dough. Press the dough squarely into the corners of the pan to avoid extra-thick edges. (The crust can be prepared 2 to 3 days ahead to this point, wrapped, and refrigerated; bring to room temperature before baking.) Put the pan on the baking sheet. Bake for 20 to 25 minutes, until the crust is fully golden brown all over. If the crust puffs up during baking, gently press it down with the back of a fork and prick it a few times.

MEANWHILE, TO MAKE THE FILLING Whisk the 3 eggs with the sugar, salt, and vanilla in a medium bowl. Whisk in the sour cream.

When the crust is ready, remove it from the oven and turn the temperature down to 300°F. Brush or spread the beaten egg yolk very thinly over the bottom of the crust to make a moisture barrier. Return the pan to the oven for 1 minute to set the egg.

Remove the crust from the oven and pour in the filling, then return the tart to the oven and bake for 15 to 20 minutes, until the filling is set around the edges but quivers like very tender Jell-O in the center when the pan is nudged. Check often in the last few minutes, as overbaking will destroy the silky-smooth texture of the filling.

Cool the tart in the pan on a rack, then refrigerate if not serving within 3 hours. If serving the tart with berries, cut the tart into wedges and garnish with spoonfuls of berries. Note that if the tart has not been refrigerated, the custard will be very soft—so spoon the berries next to each slice rather than on top of it.

CLASSIC STRAWBERRY TART

This classic French tart with a golden brown buttery crust and sweet ripe fruit over thick custard gets so very easy when you start with a press-in pastry that's mixed in minutes. And because you assemble it within hours of serving, your tart will compete with any that you can purchase. Pastry cream is just thick custard—and the perfect and classic creamy stuff under a French berry tart. It sounds fancy, but since it contains cornstarch and flour, there is no way the custard can curdle or otherwise misbehave. It's quick to make. If you won't be serving the tart within 3 to 4 hours, though, use my quick "sog-proofing" trick with a little butter, to keep the crust crisp.

Serves 8

INGREDIENTS

FOR THE PASTRY CREAM

2 tablespoons sugar

1 tablespoon unbleached all-purpose flour

1 tablespoon cornstarch

2 large egg yolks

⅔ cup whole milk

½ teaspoon pure vanilla extract

FOR THE CRUST

8 tablespoons (4 ounces) unsalted butter, melted

¼ cup (1.75 ounces) sugar

¼ teaspoon salt

¾ teaspoon pure vanilla extract

1 cup plus 2 tablespoons (5 ounces) unbleached all-purpose flour

About 2 teaspoons unsalted butter, very soft, for sog-proofing (optional)

2 pints ripe strawberries, rinsed, hulled, and halved if large

✳ VARIATIONS

Any berries can be substituted for the strawberries. Or substitute 1¼ pounds ripe figs, halved or quartered.

A Quicker Berry Tart

You can skip the pastry cream! Substitute 1 cup of mascarpone or cream cheese mixed with 4 teaspoons sugar (or more to taste) and ½ teaspoon pure vanilla extract. Proceed as directed. When serving, you might like to drizzle the slices with honey or Honey Balsamic Sauce (page 16). Try this variation with halved ripe figs instead of berries.

✳ GOOD TO KNOW

Pat the strawberries thoroughly dry before topping the tart with them.

EQUIPMENT

Medium-fine-mesh strainer

9½-inch fluted tart pan with a removable bottom

Baking sheet

DIRECTIONS

TO MAKE THE PASTRY CREAM Set the strainer over a bowl near the stove. Whisk the sugar, flour, and cornstarch together in a small bowl. Add the yolks and whisk energetically until light in color.

Heat the milk in a small heavy nonreactive saucepan until it begins to bubble at the edges. Gradually pour the hot milk into the yolk mixture, whisking constantly. Scrape the mixture back into the saucepan and cook over medium heat, stirring constantly with a silicone spatula, reaching all over the bottom and sides of the pan (especially in the corners), until the custard thickens and starts to simmer. Simmer gently, stirring constantly, for 1 minute.

Immediately scrape the custard into the strainer. Stir the custard through it, but don't press on any bits of cooked egg that may be left behind. Scrape the custard clinging to the underside of the strainer into the bowl as well. Stir in the vanilla extract. Let cool, then cover with wax paper or plastic wrap pressed directly against the surface of the custard to prevent a skin from form- ing. Refrigerate until chilled. (The pastry cream can be refrigerated for up to 3 days.)

TO MAKE THE CRUST Position a rack in the lower third of the oven and preheat the oven to 350°F.

Combine the butter, sugar, salt, and vanilla in a medium bowl. Add the flour and mix just until well blended. If the dough seems too soft and gooey, let it stand for a few minutes to firm up.

Press the dough evenly over the bottom and up the sides of the tart pan to make a thin, even layer. This takes a bit of patience, as there is just enough dough. Press the dough squarely into the corners of the pan to avoid extra-thick edges. (The crust can be prepared 2 to 3 days ahead to this point, wrapped, and refrigerated; bring to room temperature before baking.)

Put the pan on a baking sheet. Bake for 20 to 25 minutes, until the crust is fully golden brown all over. If the crust puffs up during baking, gently press it down with the back of a fork and prick it a few times. Set the pan on a rack to cool. (Once the crust is completely cool, it can be kept at room temperature, wrapped airtight, for at least 3 days.)

TO ASSEMBLE THE TART Leave the tart shell in the pan for support. If you will not be serving the tart within 3 to 4 hours, sog-proof the crust by spreading the bottom with the thinnest-possible layer of soft butter. Chill the crust to set the butter before adding the pastry cream.

Spread the pastry cream evenly in the crust. Start arranging the berries around the edges of the tart and work toward the middle. Arrange whole strawberries on the pastry cream as close together as possible, or arrange halved strawberries cut side up and overlapping. Remove the sides of the pan and transfer the tart to a serving platter. Refrigerate unless serving within 2 hours. The tart is best on the first day, but leftovers are still good on day two.

EASY BLUEBERRY TART

Something between an American pie and a French tart, the combination of raw and cooked berries (with just enough goop) in a sweet, crunchy crust appeals to everyone. A la mode is good too. The filling takes less than ten minutes to make.

Serves 8 to 10

INGREDIENTS

4 cups blueberries

Crust from Easy Lemon Tart (page 156), baked and still in the pan

¾ cup (5.25 ounces) sugar

⅓ cup water

2 tablespoons unbleached all-purpose flour

⅛ teaspoon salt

Grated zest of 1 small lemon

DIRECTIONS

Spread 2 cups of the berries in the tart crust and set aside. Combine the remaining 2 cups berries with the sugar, water, flour, salt, and lemon zest in a medium saucepan and bring to a simmer over medium heat, stirring frequently. Then simmer, stirring, until the filling is thickened and translucent, about 2 minutes.

Scrape the hot mixture into the crust, covering the raw berries, and use a fork to spread it evenly without mashing the whole berries. Let cool, then refrigerate for at least an hour, until the filling is set.

Serve the tart cold. Remove the sides of the pan and transfer the tart to a serving platter. The tart is best on the first day, but leftovers are quite good the following day.

✳ **GOOD TO KNOW**

The filling can be added to the crust when the crust is hot from the oven, warm, or even completely cooled.

BISTRO BERRY TART

Among my fondest Paris memories from the 1970s are generous slices of fresh strawberry or raspberry tart served with a big old-fashioned sugar shaker filled with slightly coarse plain white sugar. This was trendy bistro fare. The strawberries were left whole, even when large, and arranged standing up as close together as possible. Just ripe berries on a sweet, tender crust, without custard or cream underneath: a minimalist ode to good fruit. No reason not to pass a bowl of whipped crème fraîche or whipped cream, but no imperative either.

To replicate this, I use a variation of my favorite melted-butter sweet crust. It is slightly thicker with a softer crunch, from a little baking powder. Or you can use the thinner Classic Strawberry Tart crust (see page 149).

Serves 8

DIRECTIONS

Make the crust for Easy Lemon Tart on page 156. Assemble the tart after the crust is cool and a few hours before serving: Leave the tart shell in the pan for support. Arrange 2 pints of strawberries, rinsed and hulled, or 3 half pints of raspberries or blackberries, over the crust, starting from the outer edge. Remove the sides of the pan and transfer the tart to a serving platter.

Serve at room temperature. Pass servings with a shaker (or bowl) of sugar and whipped cream or whipped crème fraîche, if desired. Any leftovers can be refrigerated for the next day.

✳ VARIATIONS

If you just can't leave well enough alone, you can spread the crust with a tiny smear (just a tablespoon or so) of berry jam to make a slightly sweet liaison between the fruit and the crust.

Bistro Fig Tart

Substitute ripe figs, about 1¼ pounds, halved, for the berries, with an optional smear of fig jam (or mashed very ripe figs mixed with sugar) underneath.

EASY LEMON TART

The easiest tart crust filled with the fastest lemon curd—a go-to dessert in any season. Serve slices plain year-round, or with spoonfuls of blueberries or sliced strawberries in summer. Save leftover lemon curd to spread on your morning toast.

Serves 8 to 10

INGREDIENTS

FOR THE CRUST

10 tablespoons (5 ounces) unsalted butter, melted

¼ cup (1.75 ounces) sugar

1 teaspoon pure vanilla extract

¼ teaspoon salt

1¼ cups (5.625 ounces) unbleached all-purpose flour

¼ teaspoon baking powder

A double recipe of Lemon Curd (page 231), still hot or warm or made in advance and chilled

½ pint blueberries or raspberries or 1 pint strawberries, rinsed, hulled, and sliced (optional)

Grated lemon zest for garnish (optional)

EQUIPMENT

9½-inch fluted tart pan with a removable bottom

Baking sheet

DIRECTIONS

Position a rack in the lower third of the oven and preheat the oven to 350°F.

TO MAKE THE CRUST Combine the butter, sugar, vanilla, and salt in a medium bowl. Mix the flour and baking powder together thoroughly, add to the butter mixture, and mix just until well blended. If the dough seems too soft and gooey, let it stand for a few minutes to firm up.

Continued

※ GOOD TO KNOW

There is plenty of time to make the lemon curd while the crust is baking. But don't worry if the crust does happen to get done first: simply set it aside, leaving the oven on, until you are ready.

※ VARIATION

For an even thinner and crisper crust, substitute the crust for Classic Strawberry Tart (page 149).

Press the dough evenly over the bottom and up the sides of the tart pan to make a thin, even layer. This takes a bit of patience, as there is just enough dough. Press the dough squarely into the corners of the pan to avoid extra-thick edges. (The crust can be prepared 2 to 3 days ahead to this point, wrapped, and refrigerated; bring to room temperature before baking.)

Put the pan on a baking sheet. Bake for 20 to 25 minutes, until the crust is fully golden brown all over. If the crust puffs up during baking, gently press it down with the back of a fork and prick it a few times.

When the crust is ready, add the lemon curd (you will have some left over) and spread it evenly. Return the tart to the oven and bake for 5 minutes to set the curd (3 to 5 minutes longer if the curd was no longer hot). Let cool.

Serve the tart at room temperature or chilled (when the filling will be a little firmer), with a spoonful of berries over or alongside each slice and some lemon zest sprinkled on top, if you like. Leftovers kept in the fridge are still good the next day.

* **GOOD TO KNOW**

To remove a tart ring, set the pan on a large can and ease the sides down and off.

* **VARIATION**

Creamy Lemon Squares

Sometimes you need finger food. These are less sweet than traditional lemon bars. And very good!

Substitute an 8-by-8-inch square baking pan for the tart pan. Press the dough evenly over the bottom, but not up the sides, of the pan. Proceed as directed for Easy Lemon Tart. Chill to firm the filling, then cut into squares.

TOTALLY DOABLE MERINGUE

Meringues may sound like something only an accomplished dessert maker should attempt, but they are actually easy to make and too impressive to pass up. They keep well (for 2 weeks in an airtight container), and you can improvise dozens of spectacular desserts with them by piling on fresh ripe berries or sliced stone fruit with whipped cream or ice cream or both. The ratio of egg whites to sugar is so easy to remember that you can make meringue at the drop of a hat from any quantity of egg whites you might have on hand (see How to Make Meringue without a Recipe, page 160). Why wouldn't you want to make meringues?

6 EASY TIPS FOR PERFECT MERINGUE

1] Don't make meringue when the kitchen is super steamy or the weather is damp or humid.

2] Older egg whites work even better than fresh ones, so you can (and should!) store egg whites left over from yolky recipes in a covered glass container in the fridge, where they will keep for up to 2 weeks. Each large egg white is 2 tablespoons, so if you need 4 egg whites, you can just measure out ½ cup. You can also freeze them in ice cube trays (1 white per "cube") and store in a freezer bag or other container.

3] Egg whites beat up fluffier at room temperature, but you don't have to wait for them: simply set the bowl of cold egg whites in another bowl of hot tap water. Stir with a clean finger from time to time until the egg whites no longer feel cold (it's okay if they get slightly warm).

4] Beat egg whites in a dry stainless steel, glass, or ceramic bowl—no plastic bowls, please.

5] Regular granulated sugar is fine for most meringues, but superfine is best for the Classic Pavlova (page 161), where you want a gooey, marshmallowy interior and a crunchy crust. If you don't have superfine sugar, just process regular granulated sugar in a food processor until it's fine.

6] Now for the rule that most cooks don't know: for the fluffiest, stiffest, and most voluminous meringue, don't add the sugar too soon. Beat until the egg whites look creamy white—more like shaving cream than frothy, translucent soap suds—and you can see the tracks of the beaters on the surface. Then start adding the sugar slowly. My recipes cue you to take your time, but just think in terms of adding it a heaping teaspoon at a time, over and over again, without hesitating but not in a rush, until all the sugar is added.

That's it!

HOW TO MAKE MERINGUE WITHOUT A RECIPE

My ratio of egg whites to sugar and cream of tartar (or white vinegar) is 1 part egg whites to 2 parts sugar, plus ½ teaspoon cream of tartar or 2 teaspoons white vinegar for each cup of egg whites. Thus, for ½ cup egg whites (equivalent to 4 egg whites, and a very convenient amount for most mixers, by the way), you need 1 cup sugar and ¼ teaspoon cream of tartar or 1 teaspoon white vinegar. Easy.

TO MAKE CRUNCHY MERINGUES Position a rack in the lower third of the oven, or two racks in the upper and lower thirds, and preheat the oven to 225°F. Combine the egg whites (at room temperature) with the cream of tartar or vinegar in a clean, dry bowl. Beat at medium speed until the mixture is white and creamy and holds a soft shape when the beaters are lifted. Increase the speed to high and add the sugar a heaping teaspoon at a time, one after the other—without delay but without rushing.

Spoon the mixture onto a parchment-paper-lined baking sheet: use rounded tablespoons for cookies or spread the whole quantity into a thick layer to make a large dessert. Bake for 1½ to 2 hours. Turn the oven off and let the meringue cool inside. Once cool, meringues keep, stored airtight, for 2 weeks.

Feel free to fold ½ to ⅔ cup nuts and/or chopped chocolate and/or unsweetened or sweetened shredded dried coconut into the meringue, and/or sprinkle some on top, by eye, before you bake it. However, don't add dried fruits, because these will dry out and harden in the oven.

TO MAKE PAVLOVA MERINGUES (CRUNCHY ON THE OUTSIDE AND GOOEY WITHIN) Proceed as directed for crunchy meringues, with the following changes: Bake at 275°F on the center rack if using a single baking sheet. Use superfine sugar (or regular sugar processed in a food processor until fine). Mix 1½ teaspoons cornstarch thoroughly into each cup of sugar. Make the meringue as directed. Make dome shapes and bake as directed for Classic Pavlova (page 161) or Individual Pavlovas (page 162). Store loosely wrapped until needed. Meringue that is gooey inside keeps for a few days before it begins to dry out completely. If it does dry out, you can use it as crunchy meringue!

Additions such as nuts, chocolate, and coconut are best sprinkled over the finished dessert, when you assemble it, rather than added to the meringue batter; if sprinkled on before baking, they will burn because of the higher oven temperature.

CLASSIC PAVLOVA

Pavlova—a golden pink-hued dome of meringue slathered in whipped cream and topped with juicy ripe fruit—is a seriously underappreciated dessert. It's crunchy and gooey and sweet and creamy and tangy and saucy all at once. It's stunning to look at and unbelievably easy to make. Strawberries are a classic topping for pavlova, and they are divine, but don't hesitate to use other berries or fruits. The photograph on page 163 shows an Individual Pavlova (page 162) with sautéed nectarines before the addition of whipped cream.

Serves 6 to 8

INGREDIENTS

FOR THE MERINGUE

1 cup (7 ounces) sugar, preferably superfine

1½ teaspoons cornstarch

4 large egg whites, at room temperature

1 teaspoon distilled white vinegar or ¼ teaspoon cream of tartar

1 cup heavy cream

1 teaspoon pure vanilla extract (optional)

1½ pints strawberries, 2 half pints raspberries, blackberries, or other berries, or about 3 cups sliced peaches, nectarines, or kiwis (or a mixture)

EQUIPMENT

Food processor (optional)

Baking sheet(s)

Electric mixer (preferably a stand mixer)

DIRECTIONS

Position a rack in the center of the oven for a single large pavlova, or in the upper and lower thirds for individual pavlovas, and preheat the oven to 275°F. Trace a dark 7-inch circle on a

✳ **TIP**

Save the egg yolks to make Lemon Curd (page 231).

✳ **GOOD TO KNOW**

You can gild the lily with sauce: Purchase an extra pint of berries and puree them in a food processor. Strain and sweeten to taste if necessary (keeping it on the tart side). Spoon a little sauce over or around each serving.

✳ **VARIATIONS**

Coffee and Pineapple Pavlova

Substitute Coffee Whipped Cream (page 131) for the plain whipped cream and bite-sized pieces of fresh or grilled pineapple for the other fruit.

Rose Pavlova

Substitute Rose Whipped Cream (page 131) for the plain whipped cream and use strawberries or raspberries, or a combination.

sheet of parchment paper and flip it over on the baking sheet. Or, for individual pavlovas, line 2 baking sheets with parchment paper.

TO MAKE THE MERINGUE If your sugar is not superfine, spin it in the food processor for 15 seconds. Mix the sugar and cornstarch together thoroughly.

Combine the egg whites and the vinegar or cream of tartar in a large clean, dry bowl and beat at medium-high speed (with a stand mixer) or at high speed (with a handheld mixer) until the egg whites are creamy white and hold a soft shape when the beaters are lifted. Gradually add the sugar mixture a heaping teaspoon at a time, taking 2½ to 3 minutes in all; you should have a very stiff, creamy meringue.

For a single large pavlova, scrape the meringue onto the traced circle and use a long metal spatula or a rubber spatula to sculpt the mass into a low dome—smooth or swirly, it's up to you. Bake the pavlova for 1 hour and 15 minutes, until it is golden brown with a distinct pinkish-beige hue and feels crusty on the surface, though it will be marshmallowy inside. If it's cracked on the surface, that's okay.

For 8 individual pavlovas, scoop 4 equal portions of the meringue onto each lined baking sheet, spaced well apart. Sculpt each portion into a small dome, about 4½ inches in diameter. Bake for 1 hour, until the pavlovas are golden pink and crusty on the surface and marshmallowy within, rotating the sheets from top to bottom and front to back halfway through the baking time.

Set the baking sheet(s) on a rack to cool completely (pavlovas may sink a little). If you are not serving the pavlova(s) the same day, cover the meringue(s) loosely and leave at room temperature; it keeps for several days.

TO ASSEMBLE THE DESSERT Beat the cream, with the vanilla, if using, until it is almost stiff. Top meringues with whipped cream and garnish with the fruit.

❋ MORE VARIATIONS

Peanut Butter Pavlova

Have ready, at room temperature, ½ cup well-stirred natural, preferably salted, smooth or crunchy peanut butter; if the peanut butter is not salted, stir in a pinch of salt, or to taste. After beating the meringue, scatter small spoonfuls of the peanut butter over it and use a large rubber spatula to fold the peanut butter not quite completely into the meringue; some streaks of peanut butter should remain visible. Proceed as directed. Use strawberries for the fruit.

Hot Fudge Pavlova Sundaes

Make Individual Pavlovas. Crush in the tops with a spoon and nestle a scoop of ice cream (vanilla, coffee, coconut—your choice) in the depression in each one. Spoon on some Chocolate Sauce "to Taste" (page 23) or Cocoa Fudge Sauce (page 23) and top with sliced strawberries, whipped cream, and toasted sliced almonds.

CRUNCHY ALMOND BUTTER MERINGUE WITH BERRIES AND CREAM

Meringue laced with rich almond butter is flavorful and even more melt-in-your-mouth than plain meringue. Don't miss this sinfully simple way to serve berries and cream. Of course you can substitute hazelnut, cashew, or peanut butter and chopped nuts of the same type for the almond butter and chopped almonds.

Serves 8 to 10

INGREDIENTS

FOR THE MERINGUE

⅓ cup (3 ounces) well-stirred chunky or smooth (preferably salted) natural almond butter (see Good to Know), at room temperature

Salt (optional)

3 egg large whites, at room temperature

⅛ teaspoon cream of tartar

⅔ cup (4.625 ounces) sugar, plus more for sprinkling

¼ cup roasted almonds (plain or salted), coarsely chopped

1½ pints ripe strawberries, rinsed and hulled, or 1 pint raspberries or blackberries

Lightly Sweetened Whipped Cream (page 130)

EQUIPMENT

Baking sheet

Electric mixer (preferably a stand mixer)

DIRECTIONS

Position a rack in the lower third of the oven and preheat the oven to 225°F. Line the baking sheet with parchment paper.

By "natural" nut butter, I mean the type that contains only roasted nuts and, preferably, salt, without sugar, other sweeteners, or emulsifiers. Although the nut oil will separate in the jar, and so the nut butter must be well stirred before measuring, the flavor and consistency are better for this recipe than those of regular or "no stir" nut butters.

TO MAKE THE MERINGUE If the nut butter is not salted, stir in a pinch of salt, or to taste.

Combine the egg whites and cream of tartar in a large clean, dry bowl and beat at medium-high speed (with a stand mixer) or at high speed (with a handheld mixer) until the egg whites are creamy white and hold a soft shape when the beaters are lifted. Gradually add the sugar a heaping teaspoon at a time, taking 1½ to 2 minutes in all. The meringue should be very stiff.

Scatter small spoonfuls of the almond butter over the meringue and use a large rubber spatula to fold the almond butter not quite completely into the meringue; some streaks of almond butter should remain visible. Scrape the meringue onto the center of the lined baking sheet. With the back of a large spoon, spread the meringue into a shallow shell about 9 inches in diameter, with slightly raised edges. Sprinkle the edges with the almonds.

Bake for 2 hours. Turn the oven off and leave the meringue in the oven to cool. (Once it is completely cool, the meringue can be stored in an airtight container for at least 2 weeks.)

TO ASSEMBLE THE DESSERT Cut the strawberries in half, or into quarters if they are very large, and toss them with a sprinkling of sugar to taste. Spoon the whipped cream over the meringue, leaving the edges showing. Top with the berries and serve.

COCONUT MERINGUE
WITH PINEAPPLE AND CREAM

You can streamline the recipe by skipping the coconut-toasting step. And you can substitute 1½ pints of strawberries or raspberries for the pineapple.

Serves 8 to 10

INGREDIENTS

FOR THE MERINGUE

½ cup (1.5 ounces) unsweetened, shredded dried coconut

⅔ cup (4.625 ounces) sugar

3 large egg whites

⅛ teaspoon cream of tartar

⅓ cup (.5 ounce) unsweetened coconut chips (see Ingredients, page 270), optional

¼ to ⅓ fresh pineapple

Lightly Sweetened Whipped Cream (page 130)

EQUIPMENT

Baking sheet

Electric mixer (preferably a stand mixer)

DIRECTIONS

Position a rack in the center of the oven and preheat the oven to 300°F. Line the baking sheet with parchment paper.

TO MAKE THE MERINGUE Set a medium bowl near the stove. Spread the coconut in a wide heavy skillet and stir constantly over medium heat until the coconut begins to color slightly. Turn the heat down and continue to stir until the coconut approaches golden brown. Lift the

* VARIATION

If you happen to be grilling anyway, you can grill the pineapple slices until they start to turn golden brown. Let them cool before cutting them into pieces and assembling the dessert. Grilled or not, you can toss the pieces with a tablespoon or two of rum or bourbon.

pan off the heat and continue to stir, letting the residual heat of the pan finish toasting the coconut slowly and evenly. The whole process takes less than 5 minutes.

Scrape the coconut into the bowl and stir in 3 tablespoons of the sugar. Set aside.

Combine the egg whites and cream of tartar in a large clean, dry bowl and beat at medium-high speed (with a stand mixer) or at high speed (with a handheld mixer) until the egg whites are creamy white and hold a soft shape when the beaters are lifted. Gradually add the remaining sugar a heaping teaspoon at a time, taking 1½ to 2 minutes in all. The meringue should be very stiff.

Use a large rubber spatula to fold the toasted coconut into the meringue, just until incorporated. Scrape the meringue onto the center of the lined baking sheet. With the back of a large spoon, spread the meringue into a shallow shell about 9 inches in diameter, with slightly raised edges. Sprinkle the edges with the coconut chips, if using.

Bake for 10 to 15 minutes, until the meringue—or the shaved coconut chips, if using—begins to turn golden, whichever happens first. Turn the oven down to 200°F and continue to bake for a total of 2 hours. Turn the oven off and leave the meringue inside the oven to cool. (Once it is completely cool, the meringue can be stored in an airtight container for at least 2 weeks.)

TO ASSEMBLE THE DESSERT You can prepare the pineapple and whipped cream ahead and refrigerate them separately and assemble the dessert at the last minute. Or you can assemble the dessert up to 3 hours ahead and refrigerate it, in which case the meringue will start to soften and merge with the cream. Both ways are good. Peel and core the pineapple and cut into small wedges or fans.

Spoon the cream over the meringue, leaving the edges showing, and top with the pineapple. Serve, or refrigerate for up to 3 hours.

✳ VARIATION
Coconut Meringue Cookies

These sweet, flavorful cookies are wildly versatile. Just enjoy them, or assemble dreamy individual desserts by nestling a couple with whipped cream and berries, sliced bananas or mangoes, or even grilled pineapple slices.

Position oven racks in the upper and lower thirds of the oven. Line two baking sheets with parchment paper. Mix the batter as directed for the Coconut Meringue. Drop heaping teaspoons of batter 2 inches apart on the lined baking sheets. Sprinkle each with coconut chips. Bake as directed, but rotate the sheets from top to bottom and front to back halfway through the first baking period so that the meringues brown evenly. Continue as directed for the Coconut Meringue. (Makes 25 to 30 cookies.)

LICKETY-SPLIT CAKES

Here is a collection of cakes and tortes that are versatile and quick to make when you want something simple but homemade—when you want a slice to soak up the juices of fresh berries and cream, or something to slather with chocolate. Many are so simple and flavorful and moist that frosting or filling is not needed. A dollop of whipped cream might be the only thing that can make them even more fabulous. Most of them are one-bowl recipes, or cakes with batters mixed in the food processor (lickety-split); some are iconic tortes that I've modernized or even just reorganized to simplify (as in, why didn't I think of that before?) in order to get the same (or better) results more easily, and with guaranteed perfection every time. Nothing fiddly here.

MINI CAKE TUTORIAL

Here is the short list of what matters when you bake a cake.

POSITIONING THE OVEN RACKS

Ovens (like rooms) are hotter at the top than at the bottom. Most cakes are best baked on a rack just below the center—aka in the lower third of the oven. Cakes baked in the top half of the oven may not rise as high as they should and may be overbrowned on top and undercooked within. If you must bake cake layers on two different racks, position the racks in the upper and lower thirds of the oven and rotate the pans (from the top to the bottom and front to back) halfway through the baking time for even baking. I know it may sound fussy, but if you have often been unsatisfied with the results of your baking, this kind of fussing may make all the difference.

PREHEATING THE OVEN

Preheat the oven for at least 15 minutes before you bake. These recipes were developed and tested in a conventional oven. To bake in a convection oven, check your oven's operating manual for instructions: it may tell you to bake at a temperature 25 degrees lower than the recipe calls for and to check for doneness a little bit early.

CHOOSING THE RIGHT PANS

You will get the best results if you use the same type of pan (metal or glass) and the same size called for in the recipe. It may be hard to fathom that a 9-inch pan will produce quite different results from an 8-inch pan, but it will. A 9-inch round pan has 25 percent more surface area than an 8-inch round pan (and a 9-inch square pan has 25 percent more surface area than an 8-inch square pan), which means your cake will be much thinner and bake in less time than you expect. In a pinch, however, it is handy to know that a 9-inch round pan has the same area as an 8-inch square.

PREPARING THE PANS

Cake pan sides may be ungreased, greased, or greased and floured, depending on the individual recipe. Regardless, lining pan bottoms with parchment paper guarantees that your cake will never get stuck to the pan! No need to grease the paper or the pan beneath it.

INGREDIENT TEMPERATURE

Very few of the recipes in this book ask that cold ingredients be brought to room temperature, that all-important requirement of classical baking. However, when ingredient temperatures *are* specified here, it means it really does make a difference to the quality of your results.

For room-temperature eggs, leave them out of the fridge for an hour, or put whole eggs in a bowl of very warm water for a while, or break the eggs into a stainless steel bowl (which transfers heat faster than glass or crockery) and set the bowl in hot tap water. *For room-temperature milk,* measure it and leave it out of the fridge for an hour, or zap it in the microwave for a few seconds. Don't overdo it: "room temperature" is quite cool to the touch, between 68° and 70°F. *To soften butter,* leave it out on the counter until it is the right consistency, or cut it into chunks and zap it in a microwave on low for just a few seconds at a time until it feels appropriately pliable, *not* very soft or at all melted. In rethinking certain recipes so they require fewer steps (and fewer utensils), I've used some unconventional methods: for example, some recipes call for adding cold eggs, right from the fridge, to a warm batter. This trick cools the batter quickly and promotes emulsification and/or thickens the batter for better aeration as it's beaten.

HANDLING FLOUR CORRECTLY

Tough or heavy cakes are usually the result of badly measured flour (too much flour packed into the cup), of overmixing after the flour has been added, or of baking at too high or too low a temperature or for too long. Measure the flour accurately (see Measuring, page 172), mix it just enough (as called for in the recipe), check your oven temperature, and use a timer.

FOLLOWING THE RECIPE ORDER

Cakes turn out best if you move from one step to the next without delay. Gathering equipment and measuring ingredients in advance is called *mise en place* in the professional kitchen. Doing your "mise" ensures that you have everything you need so you don't have to ransack the pantry midrecipe while your butter melts, chocolate sets, or custard overcooks. *Mise en place* promotes calm in the kitchen. Who doesn't need that?

These recipes are written so that the important steps of the recipe can proceed without interruption. In many cake recipes, you'll find that the flour and other dry ingredients are blended first, although they are used later. This good habit keeps the flow of a recipe moving.

USING A THERMOMETER AND A TIMER

Arguably, one can roast a pretty good chicken at temperatures ranging from 325° to 450°F, but cakes (and cookies) are less forgiving. If you don't know how hot your oven really is, get an inexpensive oven thermometer. Take a reading in the center of the oven. And always use a timer: in a few extra minutes in the oven, a cake can go from perfect to perfectly dry. Set your timer for the shortest time called for, and add minutes as needed until your cake tests done.

USING COOLING RACKS

Cooling racks allow air to circulate underneath the item being cooled. Set cakes in their pans on a rack to cool, usually for 10 or 15 minutes, before unmolding them to finish cooling on the rack. It's good to have an extra rack for unmolding: hold the cake pan between the two racks, turn the whole business upside down, and remove the top rack and the pan. Peel the liner from the cake and flip it again between the racks to cool right side up (unless it's meant to be served upside down). Cakes should always be cooled completely before they are wrapped or enclosed in any container for storage (or they may grow mold from moisture trapped in the package).

MEASURING

Precise measuring is not critical for many of the recipes in this book: You can use a liberal hand with inclusions such as raisins, nuts, or chocolate chips to taste. And you can increase or decrease spices and flavorings to taste. But for tender cakes with a perfect crumb, and memorable cookies, carefully measuring flour and cocoa really does pay off.

THE SCOOP ABOUT MEASURING FLOUR AND COCOA WITH MEASURING CUPS

To measure 1 cup of flour or cocoa in a 1-cup dry measure: Gently loosen the flour or cocoa in the container by stirring it two or three times with a spoon. Press out any lumps of cocoa with the back of the spoon. Spoon the flour or cocoa lightly into the measure, without packing it, until it is heaped above the rim. Don't shake or tap the cup. Sweep a straight-edged knife or spatula, or your finger, across the rim of the cup to level the measure. A cup of flour will weigh about 4½ ounces; a cup of cocoa will weigh about 3¼ ounces.

None of the recipes in this collection call for measuring flour or cocoa after sifting, although some call for sifting the flour and/or cocoa with other ingredients after measuring and before incorporating it into the batter.

DRY AND LIQUID MEASURES

Dry measures are measuring cups designed specifically to measure dry ingredients. They are usually made of metal or plastic and come in sets. They are meant to be filled to the rim and leveled (see above). When using dry measures, use a ¼-cup measure to measure ¼ cup, a ½-cup measure to measure ½ cup, and so on. Liquid measures are designed to measure liquid ingredients. They are glass or clear plastic pitchers marked with measurements on the sides. To measure, set the measure on the counter—no one can hold a cup level in the air. Pour in enough liquid to come to the appropriate mark—lower your head to read the measurement at eye level.

WHY MEASURING WITH A SCALE WILL MAKE YOU HAPPY

Whether you are a novice or a professional, a scale is the quickest and easiest way of measuring when it matters. A measuring cup of flour, for example, can weigh anywhere from 4 ounces to well over 6 ounces, depending on whether the flour is compacted, loosened, or sifted; whether the cup is dipped into the flour or the flour is spooned into it; and whether the measure is leveled by tapping or shaking the cup or by sweeping a knife across the rim. But there is no need to worry about any of those details if you weigh your ingredients. You'll get more consistent results and end up with fewer dirty dishes in the bargain.

OUNCE FOR OUNCE

The ounces printed on the sides of glass measures are fluid ounces for measuring volume, not weight. A cup of any liquid is 8 fluid ounces, but a cup of raisins does not weigh the same as a cup of cornflakes. In these recipes, ounces refer to weight, not volume, unless otherwise noted. Save your glass measures for measuring liquids—never use them for measuring critical dry ingredients such as flour or cocoa.

THE BEST ONE-BOWL CHOCOLATE CAKE

Fast and easy, but good enough for company, this cake can be frosted or just dusted with a little powdered sugar. The same recipe also makes cake squares, cupcakes, or, doubled, a layer cake. And there's no need to wait for ingredients to come to room temperature or to get out the electric mixer.

Serves 8 to 10

INGREDIENTS

FOR THE CAKE

1 cup (4.5 ounces) unbleached all-purpose flour

⅓ cup plus 1 tablespoon (1.25 ounces) unsweetened natural cocoa powder

1 cup plus 2 tablespoons (7.875 ounces) granulated sugar

½ teaspoon baking soda

Rounded ¼ teaspoon salt

8 tablespoons (4 ounces) unsalted butter, melted

2 large eggs

½ cup hot water

½ teaspoon pure vanilla extract

1½ cups Chocolate Fudge Frosting (page 179) or Mocha Fudge Frosting (page 180), or powdered sugar for dusting

EQUIPMENT

8-by-2-inch round cake pan

DIRECTIONS

Position a rack in the lower third of the oven and preheat the oven to 350°F. Grease the sides of the cake pan and line the bottom with parchment paper.

✳ **GOOD TO KNOW**

Use natural, not Dutch-process, cocoa here. See the Cocoa Powder Fact Sheet on page 177 for more about choosing and using cocoa in recipes.

TO MAKE THE CAKE Whisk the flour, cocoa powder, granulated sugar, baking soda, and salt together thoroughly in a large bowl. Add the butter and eggs and whisk gently until all of the dry ingredients are moistened and the mixture resembles a very thick paste, then whisk vigorously for 30 to 40 strokes. Use a rubber spatula to stir in the hot water and vanilla, scraping the sides as necessary, just until the batter is blended and smooth. Scrape the batter into the prepared pan and spread it evenly.

Bake for 35 to 40 minutes, until a toothpick inserted in the center of the cake comes out clean. Set the pan on a rack to cool.

Slide a thin knife or a small metal spatula around the edges of the cake to detach it from the pan. Invert the cake onto the rack and peel off the parchment liner. Turn the cake right side up on the rack to cool completely. The cake keeps in an airtight container at room temperature for 3 to 4 days, or it can be frozen for up to 3 months; bring to room temperature before serving.

Frost the top and sides of the cake with the frosting, or dust with powdered sugar before serving.

❋ **VARIATIONS**

Chocolate Cake Squares

Use a 9-inch square baking pan and bake for 20 to 25 minutes. Dust the cooled cake with powdered sugar or frost it, and cut into 16 squares.

Chocolate Cupcakes

Line a 12-cup cupcake pan with paper liners. Divide the batter evenly among the cups. Bake for 18 to 22 minutes, until a toothpick inserted in the center of a couple of the cupcakes comes out clean. Set the pan on a rack to cool for 5 minutes, then remove the cupcakes and let them cool completely on the rack before frosting.

7 MORE IDEAS FOR CHOCOLATE CAKE

If you like to tinker, you can alter the flavor and texture of the cake in subtle ways with any of the following substitutions or additions:

1] For a more mellow chocolate flavor, substitute 1 cup plus 2 tablespoons (7.3 ounces) firmly packed brown sugar for the granulated sugar and/or substitute ½ cup hot low-fat or whole milk for the water, or substitute ¼ cup buttermilk for ¼ cup of the water.

2] For added flavor, substitute hot coffee or stout or coconut milk for the water.

3] For an extra-tender cake with an almond flavor, reduce the flour to ⅔ cup (3 ounces) and add ⅔ cup (2.66 ounces) almond meal (or other nut flour) with the flour; add ⅛ teaspoon pure almond extract with the vanilla.

4] For an extra-moist modern red velvet cake effect (without the traditional food coloring), add ¾ to 1 cup finely shredded raw beets to the batter at the end.

5] For a nuance of molasses flavor, reduce the sugar by 2 tablespoons and add ¼ cup molasses with the eggs.

6] For an extra-moist, soft cake, substitute 2 tablespoons flavorless vegetable oil for 2 tablespoons of the butter.

7] For extra chocolate flavor, increase the cocoa by 1 to 2 tablespoons and substitute 2 tablespoons flavorless vegetable oil for 2 tablespoons of the butter to compensate for the drying effect of the extra cocoa powder.

COCOA POWDER FACT SHEET

Natural (nonalkalized) cocoa powder is pulverized roasted and hulled cocoa beans, from which 75 to 85 percent of the fat (cocoa butter) has been removed. Dutch-process (alkalized) cocoa is further processed with a chemical alkali to reduce acidity. Alkalizing darkens the color of cocoa and alters its flavor. Some people prefer the taste of natural cocoa, while others prefer Dutch-process. It is worth tasting different cocoas (in hot cocoa or a sauce) to learn your own preference. Fans of Dutch-process cocoa prefer its rich color, toasted nutty flavor, and coffee notes, while others find the taste dull, harsh, chemical, and lacking in fruitiness. Natural cocoa tastes vibrant, fruity, and complex to its admirers, including me; detractors find it harsh, bitter, and sour! Are they interchangeable in recipes? Generally, in recipes that include leavenings such as baking powder or baking soda, you should stick with the type of cocoa called for, but absent any leavening in the recipe (such as those for brownies, sauces, fillings, etc.), it is usually fine to use the type of cocoa that tastes best to you.

MEASURING COCOA POWDER

If you haven't yet acquired a scale (the easiest way to measure dry ingredients, which may be either fluffed up or compacted, depending on how they were stored), here's how to measure cocoa powder with a measuring cup: Press out any lumps of cocoa with the back of a spoon. Gently loosen the cocoa in its container with a spoon, but avoid excessive stirring or whisking, or your measure will be too light. Spoon the cocoa lightly into the measuring cup, without packing it, until it is heaped above the rim; don't shake or tap the cup. Sweep a straight-edged knife or spatula across the rim of the cup to level the measure.

QUICK FUDGE LAYER CAKE

A fast two-layer cake to satisfy anyone in your household who wants a little more frosting with their cake!

Serves 10

INGREDIENTS

The Best One-Bowl Chocolate Cake (page 174), baked and cooled

Chocolate Fudge Frosting (opposite), Mocha Fudge Frosting (page 180), or Cocoa Fudge Sauce (page 23; cooled until thick enough to spread)

Totally Doable Chocolate Shards (page 232) made with dark chocolate (optional)

DIRECTIONS

Set the cake on a sheet of wax paper. Wrap a length of unflavored dental floss or heavy thread around the "waist" of the cake (if necessary, stick in a few toothpicks to keep the floss centered without shifting), cross the ends of the floss at the front of the cake, and then pull on the ends to cut the cake into 2 even layers. Flip the top layer, cut side up, next to the bottom.

Spread about ⅔ cup of the frosting over the bottom cake layer. Set the top layer cut side down on the frosting and frost the top and sides of the cake with the remaining frosting. Cover the frosting with chocolate shards, if using. The cake keeps under a cake dome or in an airtight container at room temperature for 3 to 4 days.

CHOCOLATE FUDGE FROSTING

Every dessert wardrobe needs options for chocolate frosting. This one, made with unsweetened chocolate, is something between ganache and fudge: it's just a tad sweeter than bittersweet ganache but not nearly as sweet as fudge. It's still very, very chocolaty and a good choice to slather on The Best One-Bowl Chocolate Cake (page 174), Chocolate Cupcakes (page 175), or One-Bowl Vanilla Cake (page 222).

Makes about 2 cups (enough to fill and frost an 8- or 9-inch layer cake or to frost a single layer or 12 cupcakes lavishly)

INGREDIENTS

4 ounces unsweetened chocolate (99% to 100% cacao), coarsely chopped

5½ tablespoons (2.75 ounces) unsalted butter, cut into small pieces

1 cup heavy cream

1 cup (7 ounces) sugar

¼ teaspoon salt

DIRECTIONS

Put the chocolate and butter in a medium heatproof bowl. Bring the cream, sugar, and salt to a simmer in a medium saucepan. Simmer for 4 minutes, stirring frequently. Pour the hot cream over the chocolate and whisk just until the chocolate is completely melted and the mixture is smooth and glossy. Set aside to cool, without stirring, for 2 to 3 hours, until the frosting is cool and thick enough to spread. Or, to speed things up, refrigerate the frosting for about 45 minutes, until cooled and thickened (but not hard), without stirring, then let it stand at room temperature until it is the desired consistency.

✳ **GOOD TO KNOW**

For the smoothest, glossiest frosting, allow it to cool and thicken slowly at room temperature (without stirring), rather than in the refrigerator, while you make and cool your cake.

MOCHA FUDGE FROSTING (OR SAUCE)

This is sweet and bittersweet at the same time, with a good hit of dark coffee flavor.

Makes about 2 cups (enough to fill and frost an 8- or 9-inch layer cake or to frost a single layer or 12 cupcakes lavishly)

INGREDIENTS

7 tablespoons (3.5 ounces) unsalted butter

1 cup (7 ounces) firmly packed brown sugar

⅔ cup (2.15 ounces) unsweetened cocoa powder, preferably natural

1½ teaspoons instant espresso powder or 2½ teaspoons freeze-dried coffee crystals

¼ teaspoon salt

⅔ cup heavy cream

1¼ teaspoons pure vanilla extract

DIRECTIONS

Melt the butter in a medium saucepan over low heat. Stir in the brown sugar, cocoa, espresso powder or coffee, and salt. Gradually stir in the cream over medium-low heat and continue to stir until the sugar dissolves and the mixture looks beautifully glossy. As soon as it starts to simmer at the edges, turn the heat down and cook at just below a simmer, stirring constantly and scraping the sides and corners of the pan to prevent scorching, for 2 minutes. Remove from the heat and stir in the vanilla.

Scrape it into a shallow bowl or (to speed the cooling) a large baking dish and refrigerate it for 1½ to 2 hours, stirring once in a while, until thickened but not too stiff. Remove from the fridge and let stand until you need it. If necessary to soften the frosting, set the bowl in a larger bowl of warm water for a few seconds and stir until it looks and feels right (or, to thicken it, refrigerate it again briefly). The sauce keeps in a covered container in the refrigerator for a week, or it can be frozen for up to 3 months; thaw in the microwave or at room temperature.

✳ GOOD TO KNOW

Cool the mixture for frosting; reheat it for sauce.

EXTRA-GOOD VANILLA FROSTING

The easiest-to-make vanilla frosting is nothing more than a one-pound box of powdered sugar mixed with a stick of softened butter and some vanilla, but this one is infinitely smoother and creamier and far more flavorful. In addition to (or instead of!) vanilla, you can add drops of almond extract, lemon or orange oil or extract, freshly grated zests, instant espresso powder, or almost anything you can think of that does not involve a lot of extra liquid. For the best results, always adjust the texture of the frosting to your liking by chilling or warming the bowl as described, rather than by adding extra sugar or liquid.

Makes about 2 cups (enough to fill and frost an 8- or 9-inch layer cake or to frost a single layer or 12 cupcakes lavishly)

INGREDIENTS

½ cup heavy cream

1 cup (7 ounces) sugar

Scant ¼ teaspoon salt, if using unsalted butter

2 teaspoons pure vanilla extract

8 tablespoons (4 ounces) unsalted or salted butter, slightly softened but still cold, cut into chunks

EQUIPMENT

Electric mixer

DIRECTIONS

Thoroughly mix the cream, sugar, and salt, if using, in a small saucepan. Wipe the sides of the pan clean with a silicone spatula and rinse the spatula (any sugar crystals clinging to it might crystallize the frosting when you use it later). Cover the pan, set over medium heat, and heat until the mixture is bubbling all over. Uncover the pan, adjust the heat so that the mixture boils actively but not too furiously, and cook, without stirring, for 1 minute. Use the spatula to scrape

* **VARIATION**

Extra-Good Vanilla Bean Frosting

Omit the vanilla extract. Split a half vanilla bean and use the point of a paring knife to scrape the seeds into the saucepan with the cream. Save the scraped pod for another use.

the hot mixture into a medium stainless steel bowl. Let cool, without stirring, until barely luke-warm, about 45 minutes.

Set the bowl in a larger bowl of cold water and ice cubes and add the vanilla to the frosting, then, with the electric mixer, gradually beat in the chunks of butter and continue to beat until the frosting is smooth and fluffy. If it is not thick or stiff enough, keep it in the ice water and continue to beat until it thickens, or chill the bowl for 15 minutes in the fridge and beat it again. Or, if the frosting is too stiff or cold, set the bowl in a larger bowl of hot water until the frosting starts to melt around the bottom, then beat it or stir briskly with a spatula until it reaches the desired consistency.

QUEEN OF SHEBA TORTE 5.0

This has been my default chocolate torte for decades now, and I continue to revise it. Version 5.0 is perfect for small kitchens and busy cooks: it's all mixed in one bowl, with the whole eggs tossed in—no separately beaten egg whites. The eggs should be cold, right out of the fridge, or the batter won't get light and fluffy. Too easy. Still elegant.

Serves 10 to 12

INGREDIENTS

½ cup (2.5 ounces) natural or blanched whole almonds, or a slightly generous ½ cup (2.5 ounces) almond meal

2 tablespoons unbleached all-purpose flour

6 ounces bittersweet chocolate (66% to 72% cacao), coarsely chopped

10 tablespoons (5 ounces) unsalted butter, softened but not super squishy, cut into chunks

¾ cup (5.25 ounces) granulated sugar

⅛ teaspoon salt

4 cold large eggs

3 tablespoons rum or brandy (optional)

⅛ teaspoon pure almond extract

Powdered sugar for dusting

Lightly Sweetened Whipped Cream (page 130), optional

EQUIPMENT

8-inch springform pan

Food processor if using whole almonds

Electric mixer

✳ GOOD TO KNOW

For the best flavor, make the torte at least a day ahead. Keep it loosely covered at room temperature.

✳ VARIATIONS

You can use different kinds of nuts (raw or toasted) and/or liquor or liqueurs. You can add the grated zest of an orange, or ¼ cup chopped dried fruits (macerated in the liqueur if you like), and generally have your way with this torte. In the old days, I flipped the torte over and poured a chocolate butter glaze or ganache over it, but now I serve it right side up with its rustic crackled, uneven surface exposed, dusted with a little powdered sugar. A big dollop of whipped cream, plain or flavored (see pages 130–133), on each serving is lovely, and fresh berries are superb as well.

DIRECTIONS

Position a rack in the lower third of the oven and preheat the oven to 375°F. Grease the bottom and sides of the springform pan.

If using whole almonds, pulse them with the flour in the food processor until finely ground. Otherwise simply mix the almond meal and flour together.

Put the chocolate in a large heatproof bowl, preferably stainless steel, set it in a wide skillet of barely simmering water (see Melting Chocolate My Way, page 97), and stir occasionally until nearly melted. Remove the bowl from the water bath and stir the chocolate until it is completely melted and smooth. Add the butter, granulated sugar, and salt and beat with the electric mixer at medium speed until the butter is completely melted and the mixture thickens and lightens slightly in color. Beat in the eggs one by one, followed by the liquor, if using, and almond extract. Continue beating at high speed (medium speed in a heavy-duty stand mixer) for a minute or two, or until the batter is fluffy and lightened in color. Stir in the almond mixture.

Scrape the batter into the prepared pan and spread it evenly. Bake for 30 to 35 minutes, until a toothpick inserted in the center of the torte comes out with a few moist crumbs.

Set the pan on a rack to cool. Slide a thin knife or small metal spatula around the inside of the pan to loosen the cake and allow the thin crust on top to sink (slightly) as the cake cools. Let cool completely. Remove the pan sides and transfer the cake to a serving platter. The torte can be kept at room temperature, covered or under a cake dome, for at least 3 days, or frozen, well wrapped, for up to 3 months; bring to room temperature before serving.

Sift a little powdered sugar over the top to highlight the crackled surface. Serve slices with a dollop of whipped cream, if desired.

EXTRA VIRGIN CHOCOLATE ALMOND TORTE

The flavors of fragrant olive oil and dark chocolate in this otherwise classic torte will surprise and delight you. Inspired by writer, olive oil expert, and friend Fran Gage, I created the recipe originally for the California Olive Ranch to celebrate the 2009 harvest. Don't make the mistake of thinking that olive oil for desserts should always be mild or bland—I like to use a delicious flavorful oil and celebrate its affinity with the chocolate, rather than try to hide it. If possible, bake the torte a day ahead to allow flavors to develop.

Serves 12

INGREDIENTS

Scant ½ cup (2 ounces) natural or blanched whole almonds, or ½ cup (2 ounces) almond meal

2 tablespoons unbleached all-purpose flour

6 ounces bittersweet chocolate (70% to 72% cacao), coarsely chopped

½ cup flavorful extra virgin olive oil, plus more for drizzling

⅛ teaspoon fine sea salt

4 large eggs, separated, at room temperature

¾ cup (5.25 ounces) sugar

⅛ teaspoon cream of tartar

Flaky sea salt, such as fleur de sel

EQUIPMENT

8-inch springform pan

Food processor if using whole almonds

Electric mixer

DIRECTIONS

Position a rack in the lower third of the oven and preheat the oven to 375°F. Grease the bottom and sides of the springform pan with olive oil.

If using whole almonds, pulse them with the flour in the food processor until finely ground. Otherwise simply mix the almond meal and flour together.

Put the chocolate, olive oil, and fine sea salt in a large heatproof bowl, preferably stainless steel, set it in a wide skillet of barely simmering water (see Melting Chocolate My Way, page 97), and stir occasionally until the chocolate is nearly melted. Remove the bowl from the heat and stir the chocolate until it is completely melted and smooth. Whisk in the egg yolks and ½ cup of the sugar. Set aside.

With the electric mixer, beat the egg whites and cream of tartar in a clean, dry bowl at medium speed until soft peaks form when the beaters are lifted. Gradually sprinkle in the remaining ¼ cup sugar, then beat at high speed until the egg whites are stiff but not dry.

Use a large rubber spatula to fold one-quarter of the egg whites into the chocolate mixture. Scrape the remaining egg whites into the bowl, pour the almond mixture on top, and fold just until the egg whites and almonds are evenly incorporated. Scrape the batter into the prepared pan and spread it evenly. Bake for 25 to 30 minutes, until a toothpick inserted in the center of the torte comes out with a few moist crumbs.

Set the pan on a rack to cool. Slide a thin knife or a small metal spatula around the inside of the pan to loosen the cake and allow the thin crust on top to sink (slightly) as the cake cools. Let cool completely. Remove the pan sides and transfer the cake to a serving platter. The torte can be kept at room temperature, covered or under a cake dome, for at least 3 days, or frozen, well wrapped, for up to 3 months; bring to room temperature before serving. Serve slices with a drizzle of olive oil and a few flakes of flaky sea salt.

CHOCOLATE PECAN TORTE

There are lots of toasted pecans in this all-in-one-bowl bittersweet chocolate torte. It's good on its own, but I often pass a bowl of plain whipped cream; Mocha or Milk Chocolate Whipped Cream (page 131 or 133) are also good here. For the best flavor (and convenience!), make the torte at least a day, if not two, ahead.

Serves 10 to 12

INGREDIENTS

1 cup (3.5 ounces) pecan halves

2 tablespoons unbleached all-purpose flour

6 ounces bittersweet chocolate (66% to 72% cacao), coarsely chopped

8 tablespoons (4 ounces) unsalted butter, softened but still cool, cut into chunks

¾ cup (5.25 ounces) granulated sugar

Generous ⅛ teaspoon salt

4 cold large eggs

Powdered sugar for dusting

Lightly Sweetened Whipped Cream (page 130), optional

EQUIPMENT

8-inch springform pan

Baking sheet

Food processor

Electric mixer

DIRECTIONS

Position a rack in the lower third of the oven and preheat the oven to 350°F. Grease the bottom and sides of the springform pan.

Continued

Toasted walnuts or hazelnuts (with the skins rubbed off) make a nice changeup for the pecans. You can grate the zest of 1 orange into the batter, if you like; then stir it in. Top each slice with whipped cream (plain, mocha, or white chocolate— see pages 130–133) and grate a little cinnamon stick over the top of the cake and cream. In addition to the cinnamon, try a pinch of ground ancho or other chile.

Flourless Chocolate Pecan Torte

You can simply omit the flour, without substituting anything for it, or you can increase the nuts by an ounce or so. The texture of the torte will be a bit nubbier, as the flour provides a little creaminess.

Spread the pecans on the baking sheet and bake them for 7 to 10 minutes, stirring once or twice, until they are fragrant and taste toasty. Scrape the nuts onto a plate and let cool completely. Turn the oven temperature up to 375°F.

Pulse the pecans with the flour in the food processor until finely ground.

Put the chocolate in a large heatproof bowl, preferably stainless steel, set it in a wide skillet of barely simmering water (see Melting Chocolate My Way, page 97), and stir occasionally until nearly melted. Remove the bowl from the water bath and stir the chocolate until it is completely melted and smooth.

Add the butter, granulated sugar, and salt and beat with the electric mixer at medium speed until the butter is completely melted and the mixture thickens and lightens slightly in color. Beat in the eggs one by one, then beat at high speed (medium speed in a heavy-duty stand mixer) for a minute or two, or until the batter is fluffy and lightened in color. Stir in the pecan mixture.

Scrape the batter into the prepared pan and spread it evenly. Bake for 30 to 35 minutes, until a toothpick inserted about 1½ inches from the side of the pan comes out clean; the center will still be gooey.

Set the pan on a rack to cool. Slide a thin knife or a small metal spatula around the inside of the pan to loosen the cake and allow the thin crust on top to sink (slightly) as the cake cools. Let cool completely. Remove the pan sides and transfer the cake to a serving platter. The torte can be kept at room temperature, covered or under a cake dome, for at least 3 days, or frozen, well wrapped, for up to 3 months; bring to room temperature before serving.

Sift a little powdered sugar over the top to highlight the crackled surface. Serve slices with a dollop of whipped cream, if desired.

MY FAVORITE FLOURLESS CHOCOLATE CAKE

Every dessert repertoire needs an unrelentingly rich chocolate recipe of this type: butter, eggs, and chocolate—lots and lots of chocolate. Iconic accompaniments include the yin-yang of a tangy berry sauce and whipped cream; I sometimes top the whipped cream garnish with a few pomegranate seeds.

Serves 12

INGREDIENTS

1 pound bittersweet or semisweet chocolate (55% to 70% cacao), coarsely chopped

½ pound (8 ounces) unsalted butter, cut into chunks

8 cold large eggs

¼ teaspoon salt

Powdered sugar or cocoa powder for dusting (optional)

Fresh ripe berries, Raspberry Blackberry Puree (page 81), or Saucy Berries (page 81), optional

Lightly Sweetened Whipped Cream (page 130), optional

EQUIPMENT

8-inch springform pan

Large baking or roasting pan

Electric mixer

Instant-read thermometer

DIRECTIONS

Position a rack in the lower third of the oven and preheat the oven to 325°F. Line the bottom of the springform pan with parchment paper and grease the sides. Put the pan on a large sheet of heavy-duty foil and wrap the foil up around the sides without tearing it. Set the pan in the baking or roasting pan. Bring a kettle of water to a boil.

Put the chocolate and butter in a large heatproof bowl, preferably stainless steel, set it in a wide skillet of barely simmering water (see Melting Chocolate My Way, page 97), and stir frequently until the chocolate and butter are melted and the mixture is smooth and warm. Remove the bowl from the water bath.

Meanwhile, using the electric mixer, beat the eggs with the salt in a medium bowl at high speed (medium-high speed in a heavy-duty stand mixer) for 5 minutes until the volume of the eggs doubles. With a large rubber spatula, fold one-third of the beaten eggs into the chocolate mixture until just a few streaks of egg are still visible. Fold in half of the remaining eggs likewise, then fold in the remaining eggs until completely incorporated.

Scrape the batter into the prepared pan and smooth the surface. Set the pan, in the baking pan, on the oven rack and pour enough boiling water into the larger pan to come about halfway up the sides of the springform pan. Bake for 20 to 25 minutes, until the cake has risen slightly, the edges are just beginning to set, and a thin, shiny crust (like on brownies) has formed; an instant-read thermometer inserted halfway into the center of the cake should register 140°F. Remove the pan from the water bath, set it on a rack, and let cool to room temperature, then cover the cake and refrigerate, preferably overnight, to mellow the flavor. Slide a thin knife or a small metal spatula around the sides of the cake to release it from the pan. Remove the pan sides, invert the cake onto a sheet of wax paper, and peel off the parchment liner. Turn the cake right side up on a serving platter. The cake can be kept, covered, in the refrigerator for up to 4 days, or frozen, wrapped airtight, for up to 3 months; bring to room temperature before serving.

Just before serving, dust lightly with powdered sugar or cocoa, if desired. If you like, serve with berries or berry sauce and whipped cream.

CHOCOLATE WALNUT TWEED TORTE

Loads of ground bittersweet chocolate and walnuts held together with meringue produce a moist, deceptively light cake with a speckled (tweedy) appearance and intense chocolate flavor—without flour or even egg yolks. It's perfect for Passover, and, of course, it's gluten free. I love the hint of orange zest, but you may wish to do without it. Whipped cream on top accentuates the flavor of the nuts and balances the jolt of bittersweet. Glorious, and simple as can be.

Serves 10 to 12

INGREDIENTS

1 cup (3.5 ounces) walnut pieces

½ cup plus 2 tablespoons (4.375 ounces) sugar

9 ounces bittersweet chocolate (70% to 72% cacao), coarsely chopped

Finely grated zest of 1 medium orange (optional)

⅛ teaspoon salt

1 cup egg whites (from 7 to 8 large eggs)

¼ teaspoon cream of tartar

Lightly Sweetened Whipped Cream (page 130)

EQUIPMENT

9-inch springform pan

Food processor

Electric mixer

DIRECTIONS

Position a rack in the lower third of the oven and preheat the oven to 350°F. Lightly grease the bottom and sides of the springform pan.

Continued

✳ **GOOD TO KNOW**

For success in pulverizing the nuts and chocolate, be sure that the food processor bowl and blade are perfectly dry and cool (a bowl or a blade warm from the dishwasher will melt the chocolate and turn the nuts into a paste).

Pulse the walnuts with 1 tablespoon of the sugar in the food processor until finely ground. Scrape the nuts into another bowl. Use a paper towel to wipe excess oil from the sides of the processor bowl, add the chocolate with 1 tablespoon sugar, and pulse until it forms crumbs ranging in size from coarse meal to ¼-inch bits. Add the chocolate to the nuts, along with the orange zest, if using, and salt, and stir to combine. Set aside.

Using the electric mixer, beat the egg whites with the cream of tartar in a large clean, dry bowl at medium speed until the egg whites are creamy white and soft peaks are formed when the beaters are lifted. Gradually add the remaining ½ cup sugar, beating at medium-high speed until the egg whites are glossy and stiff but not dry.

Pour half of the chocolate mixture over the egg whites and fold in with a large rubber spatula until nearly incorporated. Repeat with the remaining chocolate mixture, folding just until evenly incorporated.

Scrape the batter into the prepared pan and spread it evenly. Bake for 25 to 30 minutes, until the torte is puffed and golden brown on top and springs back when gently pressed with your fingers; a toothpick inserted in the center should come out moist and possibly stained with melted chocolate, but not coated with raw batter. Set the pan on a rack to cool. Slide a thin knife or a small metal spatula around the sides of the torte to release it from the pan. Remove the pan sides and transfer the cake to a serving platter. The torte can be kept at room temperature, covered or under a cake dome, for up to 3 days, or frozen, well wrapped, for up to 3 months; bring to room temperature before serving.

Serve slices with a dollop of whipped cream.

✳ VARIATIONS

You can substitute pecans, almonds (toasted or untoasted), or toasted and skinned hazelnuts for the walnuts. With or without the orange zest (and with any of the nut variations), you can add ⅓ to ½ cup currants that have been soaked for an hour or more in 3 tablespoons brandy, Grand Marnier, sweet Passover wine or dessert wine, vintage or tawny port, or sweet sherry. Add the currants, and any remaining liquid, to the egg whites with the second addition of the chocolate mixture.

Extra-Bittersweet Tweed Torte

Substitute 7 ounces high-quality unsweetened chocolate for the bittersweet chocolate and increase the sugar to 1 cup.

COCONUT PECAN TORTE

This simple flourless torte is moist, nicely sweet, and slightly gooey, like a macaroon. The batter is easy to make: just beat the egg whites with sugar and fold in the nuts and coconut.

Serves 10 to 12

INGREDIENTS

1⅔ cups (6 ounces) pecan halves

1½ cups (4.5 ounces) unsweetened shredded dried coconut

¾ cup plus 2 tablespoons (6.125 ounces) sugar

8 large egg whites

1 teaspoon pure vanilla extract

¼ teaspoon cream of tartar

½ teaspoon salt

Lightly Sweetened Whipped Cream (page 130), optional

EQUIPMENT

9-inch springform pan

Baking sheet

Food processor

Electric mixer

DIRECTIONS

Position a rack in the lower third of the oven and preheat the oven to 325°F. Grease the bottom and sides of the springform pan.

Spread the pecans on the baking sheet and bake them for 7 to 10 minutes, stirring once or twice, until they are fragrant and taste toasty. Scrape the nuts onto a plate and let cool completely. Turn the oven temperature up to 350°F.

Continued

Pulse the pecans and coconut with ¼ cup of the sugar in the food processor until they have the consistency of crumbs. Set aside.

Using the electric mixer, beat the egg whites, vanilla, and cream of tartar in a large clean, dry bowl at medium-high speed until the egg whites are creamy white and hold a soft shape. Mix the salt with the remaining ½ cup plus 2 tablespoons sugar and gradually add it to the egg whites, beating at high speed until the egg whites are glossy and stiff but not dry.

Pour half of the coconut mixture over the egg whites and fold in with a large rubber spatula until partially incorporated. Add the rest of the coconut mixture and fold just until incorporated.

Scrape the batter into the prepared pan and spread it evenly. Bake for 25 to 30 minutes, until the torte is puffed and golden and the edges are just barely starting to shrink from the sides of the pan. Set the pan on a rack to cool. Slide a thin knife around the inside of the pan to loosen the cake. Remove the pan sides and transfer the cake to a serving platter. The torte can be kept at room temperature, covered or under a cake dome, for 3 to 4 days, or frozen, well wrapped, for up to 3 months; bring to room temperature before serving.

If desired, serve each slice with a dollop of whipped cream.

✳ VARIATION

In season, you can garnish each serving with sliced ripe strawberries, peaches or nectarines, or grilled pineapple fans.

OLIVE OIL POUND CAKE

This is a simple basic cake for olive oil lovers. Any extra virgin olive oil you like—from delicate to robust—will be good in the cake. Feel free to make it a day ahead. It keeps well for days, and slices taste good toasted too.

Serves 16 to 20

INGREDIENTS

3 cups (13.5 ounces) unbleached all-purpose flour

2 teaspoons baking powder

2 cups (14 ounces) sugar

¼ teaspoon salt

1 cup flavorful extra virgin olive oil

1 teaspoon pure vanilla extract

5 cold large eggs

1 cup whole milk

EQUIPMENT

10- to 12-cup tube or Bundt pan or two 8-by-4-inch loaf pans

Electric mixer

DIRECTIONS

Position a rack in the lower third of the oven and preheat the oven to 350°F. Grease and flour the pan(s), or line the bottom and sides of the loaf pans with parchment paper.

Sift the flour and baking powder together. Set aside.

Using the electric mixer, beat the sugar, salt, oil, and vanilla in a large clean, dry bowl until well blended. Add the eggs one at a time, beating well after each addition, then continue to beat until the mixture is thick and pale, 3 to 5 minutes. Add one-third of the flour mixture and

* **VARIATION**

Olive Oil Cake with Saffron and Cardamom

Sprinkle a scant ¼ teaspoon crushed or chopped saffron threads over the milk; let stand for 10 minutes. Crack open 7 whole cardamom pods, pick out the seeds, and crush them in a mortar or a spice grinder; add them with the sugar. Or add ½ teaspoon ground cardamom.

beat at low speed just until blended. Add half of the milk and beat just until blended. Repeat with another third of the flour, the remaining milk, and then the remaining flour.

Scrape the batter into the pan(s). Bake for 1 hour to 1 hour and 10 minutes, until a cake tester inserted in the center of the cake comes out clean. Cool in the pan(s) on a rack for about 15 minutes.

If using a tube or Bundt pan, slide a skewer around the tube, then slide a thin knife around the edges of the pan to release the cake, invert the pan, and then turn the cake right side up on a rack to cool completely. Or slide a thin knife around the sides of the loaf pans (unless they are lined with parchment paper), invert the cakes, and turn right side up to cool on the rack. Once cooled, the cake keeps well at room temperature, wrapped airtight, for at least 3 days, or in the freezer for up to 3 months; bring to room temperature before serving.

* TIP

Lining loaf pans with parchment paper eliminates the need for greasing and prevents the bottoms and sides of the loaves from overbrowning.

Turn a pan upside down on the counter and center a 6-by-12-inch piece of parchment on it. Fold the paper down against all four sides of the pan and crease the folds. Overlap the corner "wings" against the ends of the pan, creasing the folds. Remove the paper and insert it into the pan, adjusting the folds and creases.

ALMOND CAKE

Rich and buttery with big almond flavor, this cake is mixed in seconds in a food processor, but it tastes fancy and sophisticated, and it keeps for days. Serve it solo with great coffee, or garnish it with fresh fruit, Raspberry Blackberry Puree (page 81) or Saucy Berries (page 81), poached pears in wine, or any of the cherry compotes (pages 54–55). See the many variations that follow for more reasons to make it again. The flavor and texture are best if you bake the cake at least a day before serving.

Serves 10 to 12

INGREDIENTS

¾ cup plus 2 tablespoons (4.375 ounces) unblanched or blanched whole almonds

1 cup plus 2 tablespoons (7.875 ounces) granulated sugar

¼ teaspoon salt

½ teaspoon pure almond extract

8 tablespoons (4 ounces) unsalted butter, cut into chunks and slightly softened

1 tablespoon kirsch (optional)

3 large eggs

⅓ cup (1.5 ounces) unbleached all-purpose flour

¼ teaspoon baking powder

Powdered sugar for dusting (optional)

EQUIPMENT

8-by-2-inch round cake pan

Food processor

DIRECTIONS

Position a rack in the lower third of the oven and preheat the oven to 350°F. Butter the sides of the cake pan and line the bottom with parchment paper.

Put the almonds, granulated sugar, salt, and almond extract in the food processor and process until the nuts are finely pulverized. Add the butter and kirsch, if using, and pulse until blended. Add the eggs and process until thoroughly blended. Add the flour and baking powder and pulse just until incorporated, scraping the bowl once with a rubber spatula to be sure.

Scrape the batter into the prepared pan and spread it evenly. Bake for 35 to 40 minutes, until the cake is golden brown on top and a toothpick inserted in the center comes out clean. Cool completely in the pan on a rack.

To unmold, slide a thin knife or a small metal spatula around the sides of the cake to release it. Cover the cake with a serving platter and invert. Remove the pan, peel off the parchment liner, and turn the cake right side up. Wrapped airtight, the cake keeps well at room temperature for several days, or in the freezer for up to 3 months; bring to room temperature before serving.

If desired, dust the cake lightly with powdered sugar before serving.

✳ VARIATIONS

ORANGE-SCENTED ALMOND CAKE Add the grated zest of 1 medium orange to the food processor with the almonds. Reduce the almond extract to ¼ teaspoon. Omit the optional kirsch and add 1 teaspoon orange flower water with the butter.

ROSE-SCENTED ALMOND CAKE Reduce the almond extract to ¼ teaspoon. Omit the optional kirsch and add 2 teaspoons rose water with the butter.

LEMON-AND-CINNAMON-SCENTED ALMOND CAKE Add the grated zest of 1½ small lemons and a scant ½ teaspoon ground cinnamon to the food processor with the almonds. Reduce the almond extract to ¼ teaspoon and omit the optional kirsch.

CARDAMOM ALMOND CAKE Add ½ teaspoon ground cardamom to the food processor with the almonds. Reduce the almond extract to ¼ teaspoon and omit the optional kirsch.

HAZELNUT CAKE, WITH OPTIONS Substitute ¾ cup plus 2 tablespoons (4 ounces) hazelnuts, blanched or unblanched, for the almonds. Omit the almond extract and optional kirsch. If desired, add 1 tablespoon Frangelico, or 1 teaspoon rose water, or 1 teaspoon orange blossom water plus the finely grated zest of 1 orange to the food processor with the nuts.

CARROT ALMOND TORTE

This is *not* the ubiquitous American cake flecked with shredded carrots, laced with chopped walnuts and crushed pineapple, and slathered with cream cheese frosting—it is something else entirely. Adapted (considerably!) from a recipe in the 1948 *Settlement Cookbook,* it is a moist and sophisticated flourless torte made almost entirely of egg whites, almonds, and carrots. It is divine. You will find a superb version of that other carrot cake on page 209. You can make this cake a day or two in advance.

Serves 10 to 12

INGREDIENTS

1½ cups (7.5 ounces) unblanched whole almonds

¾ cup plus 2 tablespoons (6.125 ounces) sugar

2 cups (8 ounces) lightly packed finely grated peeled carrots

1 medium orange

4 large eggs, separated, at room temperature

¼ teaspoon salt

Slightly rounded ½ teaspoon ground cinnamon

¼ teaspoon pure almond extract

⅛ teaspoon cream of tartar

Unsweetened Whipped Cream (page 130; with a little vanilla, if you like) or mascarpone (optional)

EQUIPMENT

8-inch springform pan

Food processor

Microplane zester

Electric mixer

✱ TIPS

Beat egg whites at room temperature in a grease-free stainless steel or glass bowl (no plastic bowls, please!).

In a hurry? You can put cold eggs in hot tap water for a few minutes before you crack them, or set the bowl of egg whites in a pan of hot tap water and stir with a clean finger until they no longer feel cold.

DIRECTIONS

Position a rack in the lower third of the oven and preheat the oven to 325°F. Butter or grease the bottom and sides of the springform pan.

Pulse the almonds with 2 tablespoons of the sugar in the food processor until very finely ground. Set aside.

Stack three or four paper towels on the counter. A handful at a time, squeeze the grated carrots hard to extract as much juice as possible, and put each handful in the center of the paper towels. (Sip or discard the carrot juice.) Gather the edges of the towels up around the carrots and squeeze again. Set aside.

Use the Microplane zester to grate the orange zest into a large bowl. Add the egg yolks, salt, cinnamon, almond extract, and ½ cup plus 2 tablespoons sugar and whisk the mixture until thick and lightened in color. Sprinkle the grated carrots into the bowl, but don't mix them in.

Using the electric mixer, beat the egg whites and cream of tartar in a large clean, dry bowl at medium-high speed until the mixture is creamy white and holds a soft shape. Slowly sprinkle in the remaining 2 tablespoons sugar, beating at high speed until the egg whites are stiff but not dry. Scrape one-quarter of the egg whites on top of the carrots and use a rubber spatula to fold them into the batter. Scrape the remaining egg whites into the bowl, pour the ground almonds over them, and fold them in. Scrape the batter into the prepared pan and spread it evenly.

Bake for 45 to 50 minutes, until the top of the torte is golden brown and just beginning to separate from the sides of the pan and the torte springs back when you press it gently with a finger. Cool the torte completely in the pan on a rack.

Slide a thin knife or a small metal spatula around the sides of the torte to detach it from the pan. Remove the pan sides and transfer the cake to a serving platter. The cake keeps under a cake dome or in a covered container, at room temperature or in the refrigerator, for several days. Slice and serve with dollops of whipped cream or mascarpone, if desired.

CLASSIC CARROT CAKE

This little carrot cake update is not quite as oil-rich as the usual and it's a little spicier too, though not so spicy that it is a spice cake! The frosting is richly tangy and not overly sweet, a perfect partner for this lighter, brighter-tasting cake.

Serves 12

INGREDIENTS

FOR THE CAKE

1¼ cups vegetable oil

2 cups (14 ounces) sugar

4 large eggs

2 cups (9 ounces) unbleached all-purpose flour

1 teaspoon baking soda

2 teaspoons baking powder

2 teaspoons ground cinnamon

½ teaspoon ground nutmeg

¼ teaspoon ground cloves

½ teaspoon salt

3 cups (12 ounces) lightly packed grated peeled carrots

1 cup (3.5 ounces) coarsely chopped walnuts

FOR THE FROSTING

8 ounces cream cheese, slightly softened

8 tablespoons (4 ounces) unsalted butter, slightly softened

1½ cups (6 ounces) powdered sugar

½ teaspoon pure vanilla extract

✳ VARIATION

If you don't have time for frosting or don't want a sweet topping, serve the cake with a dollop of crème fraîche or mascarpone, or even plain Greek or thickened yogurt. The yin and yang of sweet cake with slightly tart topping is very appealing, but you can sweeten the toppings to taste if you like.

EQUIPMENT

9-by-13-inch baking dish

DIRECTIONS

Position a rack in the center of the oven and preheat the oven to 325°F. Grease the baking dish.

TO MAKE THE CAKE Combine the oil, sugar, and eggs in a large bowl and beat with a rubber spatula or a wooden spoon until well mixed. Add the dry ingredients and beat until smooth. Add the carrots and nuts and mix until well incorporated.

Scrape the batter into the baking dish and spread it evenly. Bake for 50 to 55 minutes, or until a toothpick inserted in the center comes out clean. Cool in the baking dish on a rack, for at least 2 hours, before frosting.

TO MAKE THE FROSTING Combine all the ingredients in a medium bowl and mix by hand or with an electric mixer just until smooth.

TO ASSEMBLE THE CAKE Drop dollops of frosting all over the top of the cake, then spread evenly with a small spatula or the back of a clean wooden spoon. Cover and refrigerate the cake until ready to serve. The cake keeps for up to 5 days; bring to room temperature before serving. Cut into 3-inch squares to serve.

✳ GOOD TO KNOW
5 More Things to Do with Carrot Cake

1] Substitute 3 cups grated raw peeled yam or winter squash (such as butternut) for the grated carrots.

2] Use generous measures of the spices for an extra-spicy cake.

3] Add up to a cup of raisins or chopped dried fruit with the nuts.

4] Add a teaspoon of ground ginger and/or ¼ cup finely diced candied ginger.

5] Grate the zest of an orange or a lemon into the bowl with the other ingredients.

A JOLT OF GINGER

Ginger adds a hot, fresh, palate-tingling flavor to any dish.

Ground dried ginger is the familiar pale yellow powder in a jar. It is very pungent and earthy, and it has a more peppery flavor than fresh ginger.

Fresh ginger is available in the produce section of specialty markets and many supermarkets. It looks like a knobby root (it is actually a rhizome, or tuber-like stem) with a papery brown skin. Fresh ginger has a brighter, tarter, and more citrusy flavor than ground dried ginger. Choose tubers that feel heavy for their size, rather than light (which indicates that they have lost a lot of their natural moisture). Look for taut, smooth skin with a slight sheen. Fresh ginger keeps for at least a week, unwrapped, in a cool, dry place; it will keep for several weeks refrigerated if you wrap it first in a paper towel (to absorb moisture that might produce mold) and then enclose it in a plastic bag.

Peel fresh ginger with a vegetable peeler before slicing, grating, or pureeing. To avoid long, stringy fibers, thinly slice the ginger across the grain before chopping, mincing, or pureeing.

Crystallized or candied ginger is cooked in a syrup and sugar coated, and it is a delicious candy just as it comes. Chopped or minced, it makes a great addition to cookies, muffins, and pound cakes. Crystallized or candied ginger is often available in high-end supermarkets or in shops that sell dried fruits and nuts. The Australian variety is exquisitely tender and somewhat milder than ginger from other sources (see Resources, page 277).

FRESH GINGER GINGERBREAD

Good gingerbread belongs in every cook's repertoire. This lovely, easy version is made with fresh, in addition to dried, ginger and the whole thing is mixed in a food processor. Gingerbread plays perfectly well alone (with a little powdered sugar sieved over the top for visual interest) but loves a party. For ideas, see Things to Do with Gingerbread (page 216).

Serves 8

INGREDIENTS

A piece of fresh ginger at least 3½ by 1½ inches (2.5 to 3 ounces)

⅔ cup (4.625 ounces) firmly packed light brown sugar or light muscovado sugar

1½ teaspoons ground cinnamon

1 teaspoon ground ginger

½ teaspoon ground allspice

½ teaspoon ground cardamom

¼ teaspoon salt

⅓ cup light unsulphured molasses

8 tablespoons (4 ounces) unsalted butter, melted and still warm

1 large egg

½ cup hot water

1⅔ cups (7.5 ounces) unbleached all-purpose flour

1 teaspoon baking soda

Powdered sugar for dusting and/or Lightly Sweetened Whipped Cream (page 130) or Lightly Sweetened Crème Fraîche (page 130), sour cream, or mascarpone

EQUIPMENT

8-inch square baking pan

Food processor

✳ VARIATIONS

Dark-and-Stormy Gingerbread
(photograph on page 215)

If you love the eponymous cocktail, you'll love ginger-bread laced with rum and showered with lime zest.

Substitute 3 tablespoons dark rum for 3 tablespoons of the water: measure the rum in a glass measure and then fill to the ½-cup mark with hot water. Proceed as directed. Serve the gingerbread warm; drizzle each serving with a little more rum and top with a dollop of whipped cream and a grating of lime zest.

Pantry Gingerbread

Omit the fresh ginger and increase the ground ginger to 1 tablespoon.

DIRECTIONS

Position a rack in the lower third of the oven and preheat the oven to 350°F. Grease the sides and line the bottom of the baking pan with parchment paper.

Peel the ginger with a sharp knife or a vegetable peeler. Cut the ginger crosswise into enough ¼-inch slices to measure ½ cup (or weigh 2 ounces). Add the ginger to the food processor and pulse until finely minced.

Add the brown sugar, cinnamon, ground ginger, allspice, cardamom, salt, molasses, butter, egg, water, flour, and baking soda to the processor. Process for 10 seconds. Scrape the bowl and process for 5 more seconds.

Scrape the batter into the prepared pan. Bake for 25 to 30 minutes, until the surface springs back when you press it lightly with your finger and a toothpick inserted in the center comes out clean. Cool the cake in the pan on a rack for 10 minutes.

Slide a thin knife or a small metal spatula around the sides of the cake to detach it from the pan. Invert the cake onto the rack and peel off the parchment liner. Turn the cake right side up on the rack to cool completely, or serve warm. Once cool, the cake keeps, wrapped airtight, at room temperature for 3 days, or in the freezer for up to 3 months; bring to room temperature before serving.

Serve with a dusting of powdered sugar and/or a dollop of whipped cream, crème fraîche, sour cream, or mascarpone.

THINGS TO DO WITH GINGERBREAD

Warm or at room temperature, gingerbread especially loves slightly sour or tangy accompaniments, whether creamy like crème fraîche or fruity like nectarines or pineapple. You can mix and match the ideas below.

Top with

- Crème fraîche (plain or whipped) or whipped cream.

- Mascarpone or cream cheese, or Cream Cheese Frosting (page 209).

- Greek yogurt or sour cream.

- Milk Chocolate Whipped Cream (page 133).

To any of the above, add a sprinkle of crushed Praline (page 32).

- Praline Whipped Cream (page 132).

- Lemon Whipped Cream (page 132).

- Lemon Curd (page 231).

Serve with

- Plums in Brandied Coffee Syrup (page 84).

- Apples in Cardamom Lime Syrup (page 50).

- Pears in Ginger Lemon Syrup (page 50).

- FB's Vanilla Pear and Apple Compote (page 52).

- Sliced bananas, pineapple, nectarines, or strawberries.

- Dessert Chutney (page 82).

- A drizzle of rum or brandy.

To any of the above, add a topping such as crème fraîche or mascarpone.

- Coffee or vanilla ice cream with caramel or toffee sauce.

Turn it into trifle

- In a serving bowl or in individual glasses or brandy snifters, layer cubes or slices of gingerbread, drizzled with rum or brandy, with whipped cream and lemon curd. Refrigerate for an hour or up to several hours to marry the flavors and textures.

Make an upside-down cake

- Lightly grease the sides and smear the bottom of a 9-inch round cake pan generously with 3 tablespoons soft butter. Sprinkle the bottom of the pan with ¼ cup sugar and ½ teaspoon ground cinnamon. Peel, quarter, and core a large firm ripe pear (such as Comice, Bartlett, or Bosc) and cut into ¼-inch-thick slices. Toss the pear slices in a little lemon juice and arrange them close together in a single layer over the sugar. Scatter 3 tablespoons finely diced candied ginger between the slices. Make gingerbread batter as directed and pour it over the pears. Bake as directed. Let cool for 5 minutes, then invert on a cake plate. If any of the pear slices stick to the pan, replace them on the cake.

LINZER BLITZ TORTE

This is a real linzer torte, but without the tedious lattice topping; instead, a portion of the dough is simply grated randomly over the layer of jam, using the largest holes of a box grater, or sliced into matchsticks and scattered over the jam. Expect unbelievable aromas of toasted nuts and spices when you bake this—with flavors to match. Linzer torte keeps well for at least a week, and it's as irresistible for breakfast as it is for dessert. Vanilla ice cream or the traditional whipped cream (*Schlag*) make fine partners, but a great linzer torte needs neither.

Serves 12 to 16

INGREDIENTS

¾ cup (3.75 ounces) whole almonds or hazelnuts, or a combination

1 cup (4.5 ounces) unbleached all-purpose flour

¾ cup (5.25 ounces) granulated sugar

¼ teaspoon salt

1½ teaspoons ground cinnamon

½ teaspoon ground cloves

11 tablespoons (5.5 ounces) unsalted butter, cut into chunks and slightly softened

1 large egg yolk

Grated zest of ½ lemon

Grated zest of ½ orange

¼ teaspoon pure almond extract

⅔ cup (7.33 ounces) raspberry or blackberry preserves

Powdered sugar for dusting (optional)

EQUIPMENT

Food processor

9-inch round cake pan

✳ **VARIATION**

Linzer Bars

Sometimes finger food is needed! These are good on a holiday cookie tray or sweet table.

Substitute a 9-inch square pan for the round pan. Proceed as directed for the Linzer Blitz Torte. After the torte is unmolded and turned right side up, cut it into 25 squares.

DIRECTIONS

Combine the almonds, flour, granulated sugar, salt, cinnamon, and cloves in the food processor and pulse until the almonds are finely ground. Add the butter, egg yolk, grated lemon and orange zests, and almond extract and process just until blended.

Measure ¼ cup (2.25 ounces) of the dough and shape it into a ball or a cube (if slicing). Wrap and refrigerate it.

Meanwhile, grease the sides of the cake pan and line the bottom with a circle of parchment paper. Press the remaining dough evenly over the bottom of the pan. Cover and refrigerate for at least 1 hour.

Position a rack in the lower third of the oven and preheat the oven to 350°F.

Spread the preserves evenly over the dough, leaving a scant ½-inch border all around. Using the largest holes of a box or flat grater, grate the chilled reserved dough over the jam (or cut the dough into matchsticks and scatter them over the jam).

Bake for 30 to 35 minutes, until the top is golden brown. Tent the torte loosely with foil and bake for 10 to 15 minutes longer, until it is a deep golden brown. If the torte puffs up during baking, rap the pan sharply on the oven rack to settle it. Cool the torte in the pan on a rack for 10 minutes. Slide a thin knife or a small metal spatula around the sides to release the torte. Let cool completely.

Invert the torte onto a plate. Remove the cake pan and the parchment liner, then turn the torte right side up. The torte keeps, covered, at room temperature for a good week; it can also be wrapped airtight and frozen for up to 3 months; bring to room temperature before serving.

Serve sprinkled with powdered sugar, if desired.

NUTTY SPONGE CAKE

A sponge cake is easier to make than anyone thinks it is, and it's especially worth the effort when it's flavorful enough to serve without any filling or frosting. That being said, plain whipped cream or Praline Whipped Cream (page 132), vanilla ice cream, caramel sauce, and/or berries transform it into several more desserts. The variation without nuts can also be turned into a light and lovely lemon layer cake.

Serves 10 to 12

INGREDIENTS

¾ cup (3.4 ounces) unbleached all-purpose flour

1 cup (3.5 ounces) walnut halves or pieces

1 cup (7 ounces) sugar

¼ teaspoon salt

Finely grated zest of 1 medium bright-skinned orange

2 tablespoons fresh orange juice

1 teaspoon pure vanilla extract

7 large eggs, at room temperature, separated

½ teaspoon cream of tartar

EQUIPMENT

Food processor

Electric mixer

10-inch tube pan with removable bottom, ungreased

A longneck bottle or funnel, to invert the cake onto while it cools

✳ VARIATIONS

Plain Sponge Cake

Make the cake as directed, omitting the nuts. Use a large medium-fine strainer to sift the flour into the batter as you add it.

Lemon or Berry Layer Cake

It's easy to split this tall nutty or plain sponge cake into two or even three or four layers using the dental-floss method described on page 178. You can fill the cake with whipped cream and berries, or slather the layers very generously with Lemon Curd (page 231). Either way, frost with whipped cream, or simply dust with powdered sugar just before serving. Refrigerate for at least 2 hours or up to a day ahead. Remove from the refrigerator 15 to 30 minutes before serving.

DIRECTIONS

Preheat the oven to 325°F.

Pulse the flour and nuts in the food processor until the nuts are finely ground.

Set aside 2 tablespoons of the sugar. Put the remaining sugar in a large bowl with the salt, orange zest, orange juice, vanilla, and egg yolks. Beat at high speed with the electric mixer for 3 to 5 minutes, until very thick and pale. Wash and dry the beaters.

Using the electric mixer and clean beaters, beat the egg whites with the cream of tartar in a large clean, dry bowl at medium speed until the egg whites are creamy white and soft peaks are formed when the beaters are lifted. Gradually add the reserved sugar, beating at medium-high speed until the egg whites are glossy and stiff but not dry. Scrape one-quarter of the egg whites over the yolk mixture and pour the nut mixture on top. Fold with a large rubber spatula. Scrape the remaining egg whites into the bowl and fold them in. Scrape the batter into the pan and spread it evenly.

Bake for 35 to 40 minutes, until the cake is golden brown and springy to the touch. A toothpick inserted in the cake will emerge clean. Cool in the pan, upside down on the bottle or funnel.

By the time the cake is cool it will mostly have pulled away from the sides of the pan; rap each side of the pan sharply on the counter to release any portion of the cake that is still attached to the pan. Run a skewer around the tube to detach it. Lift the tube to remove the cake. Slide a slim metal spatula around the bottom of the cake to detach it. Invert the cake onto a serving platter. The cake keeps under a cake dome or in a covered container at room temperature for 2 to 3 days; it can also be wrapped airtight and frozen for up to 3 months; bring to room temperature before serving.

ONE-BOWL VANILLA CAKE

This is my favorite all-in-one-bowl plain Jane vanilla cake. Serve it with fresh fruit, top it with vanilla or chocolate frosting, or fill it with coconut cream or lemon curd; see the recipes and variations that follow.

Serves 8 to 10

INGREDIENTS

¾ cup plus 2 tablespoons (6.125 ounces) sugar

1 cup (4.5 ounces) unbleached all-purpose flour

¼ teaspoon salt

1¼ teaspoons baking powder

⅓ cup heavy cream

3 tablespoons (1.5 ounces) unsalted butter, melted and hot, or vegetable oil

3 large eggs

2 teaspoons pure vanilla extract

EQUIPMENT

8-by-2-inch round cake pan

Food processor

DIRECTIONS

Position a rack in the lower third of the oven and preheat the oven to 350°F. Grease and flour the sides of the cake pan and line the bottom with parchment paper.

✳ GOOD TO KNOW

The oven takes longer to preheat than this batter takes to prep and mix. Gather your ingredients, but don't start actually mixing until the oven is ready!

✳ VARIATIONS

You can grate the zest of a medium orange or lemon into the bowl with the other ingredients and/or add ¼ teaspoon pure almond extract. Either way, reduce the vanilla extract to 1 teaspoon.

You can make the cake with citrus zest as described and add 3 tablespoons of poppy seeds.

Add the sugar, flour, salt, and baking powder to the food processor and pulse to blend the ingredients thoroughly. Add the cream and butter or oil and pulse quickly, 8 to 10 times, until the ingredients are blended (if you're using oil, the ingredients will be moist and beginning to clump together but not yet smooth). Add the eggs and vanilla and pulse 5 to 6 times. Scrape the sides of the bowl and pulse 5 to 6 more times, just until the ingredients are blended and smooth—no more.

Scrape the batter into the pan and spread it evenly. Bake for 30 to 35 minutes, until a toothpick inserted in the center of the cake comes out clean. Set the pan on a rack to cool for about 10 minutes.

Slide a thin knife or a small metal spatula around the edges of the cake to detach it from the pan. Invert the cake onto the rack and peel off the parchment liner. Turn the cake right side up on the rack to cool completely. Once cooled, the cake keeps, wrapped airtight, at room temperature for 3 days, or in the freezer for up to 3 months; bring to room temperature before serving.

LAYER CAKES FOR THE RELUCTANT

I hadn't planned to include layer cakes in a book dedicated to exceedingly doable desserts. But once I had a couple of great one-bowl cakes, how could I not think about simple but spectacular ways to dress them up?

For home cooks, the problem with traditional layer cakes is that they may require two or more cake pans of the same size, a large oven, and perfect timing to avoid scorching the edges of thin layers, or a skilled hand to cut a single cake into three or four impossibly thin layers, not to mention the time to make a classic cake, filling, and frosting. What to do?

My solution was to simplify every step of the way. These cakes are made in one bowl and baked in one pan. Instead of splitting them with a knife, you just wrap a length of dental floss or heavy thread around their "waist," cross the ends, and pull to make two even layers, each sturdy enough to move or lift without breaking. Layers may be drizzled with some flavorful liquid (liqueurs always work) and filled with easy but luscious stuff, like coconut whipped cream, lemon cream, or chocolate frosting. The look is casual but elegant, and the payoff for the minimal effort is high.

VERY VANILLA LAYER CAKE

A sweet little vanilla cake with yummy vanilla frosting. Serve plain or with any gorgeous red berries. In a hurry? Skip the layers; just frost the top and sides of the cake liberally.

Serves 10

INGREDIENTS

One-Bowl Vanilla Cake (page 222), baked and cooled

Extra-Good Vanilla Frosting (page 181)

Totally Doable Chocolate Shards (page 232) or Even Faster Chocolate Shavings (page 232), made with white chocolate (optional)

DIRECTIONS

Set the cake on a sheet of wax paper. Wrap a length of unflavored dental floss or heavy thread around the "waist" of the cake (if necessary, stick in a few toothpicks to keep the floss centered without shifting), cross the ends of the floss at the front of the cake, and then pull on the ends to cut the cake into 2 even layers. Flip the top layer, cut side up, next to the bottom layer.

Spread about ⅔ cup of the frosting over the bottom cake layer. Set the top layer cut side down on the frosting and frost the top and sides of the cake with the remaining frosting. Cover the frosting with chocolate shards, if using. The cake keeps under a cake dome or in an airtight container at room temperature for 3 to 4 days.

✳ **VARIATION**

Chocolate Layer Cake

For old-fashioned types who remember when a chocolate layer cake meant vanilla cake with chocolate frosting, substitute Mocha Fudge Frosting (page 180) or Chocolate Fudge Frosting (page 179). Make the shards, if using, with dark chocolate.

COCONUT LAYER CAKE

Here's an easy, fresh-tasting, flavorful, boozy layer cake that is appreciated by coconut lovers and a surprising number of (surprised) coconut haters as well. Cracking a fresh coconut and wrestling the meat from its shell is fun, but not easy. The beauty of this cake is that it tastes as if it's made with fresh coconut, yet it's not. The secret? The cream for the filling is intentionally underwhipped, leaving plenty of moisture to hydrate the dried coconut so it tastes like fresh.

Serves 10

INGREDIENTS

2 tablespoons fresh lemon juice

¼ cup dark rum

3½ teaspoons granulated sugar

2 tablespoons water

1 cup heavy cream

⅔ cup (2 ounces) unsweetened shredded dried coconut

One-Bowl Vanilla Cake (page 222), baked and cooled

Generous ¼ cup apricot jam (mash or cut up any extra-large chunks)

Powdered sugar for dusting

Unsweetened coconut chips for garnish (optional)

DIRECTIONS

Combine the lemon juice, rum, 1½ teaspoons of the granulated sugar, and the water in a cup or a small bowl and stir to dissolve the sugar.

Whip the cream with the remaining 2 teaspoons granulated sugar just until it holds a very soft shape: it should seem underwhipped, not even close to stiff, or your filling will be dry and crumbly rather than soft and moist. Fold in the coconut and set aside.

Continued

* **GOOD TO KNOW**

You can fool around with the booze and lemon mixture and jam, swapping in other types and flavors. Consider using tequila instead of rum and replacing the lemon juice and water with 6 tablespoons of fresh orange juice. Or substitute brandy or bourbon for the rum and 6 tablespoons strong coffee or espresso for the lemon juice and water.

You can omit the jam entirely.

If you have an extra lemon, lime, or orange, grate a little zest over the cake just before serving for a burst of fragrance.

Set the cake on a sheet of wax paper. Wrap a length of unflavored dental floss or heavy thread around the "waist" of the cake (if necessary, stick in a few toothpicks to keep the floss centered without shifting), cross the ends of the floss at the front of the cake, and then pull on the ends to cut the cake into 2 even layers. Flip the top layer, cut side up, next to the bottom layer.

Drizzle the cut side of each layer with one-third of the rum mixture. Spread the jam over the bottom layer. Spread the coconut-cream mixture on top of the jam—this will make a very thick layer of filling. Turn the top layer moist side down on top of the filling. Drizzle the cake with the rest of the rum mixture. If the cake is uneven, leaning, or tilted, use your hands to press or push it gently into shape.

Refrigerate the cake under a bowl or in a covered container for at least several hours, or up to a day, to allow the cake and coconut to absorb moisture and flavors.

Remove the cake from the refrigerator 30 to 60 minutes before serving. Sift a little powdered sugar over the top of the cake just before serving and garnish with coconut chips, if desired.

✳ VARIATIONS

Coconut Layer Cake with Lime

Omit the apricot jam and replace the lemon juice with fresh lime juice. Grate a little lime zest over the top of the cake just before serving.

Frosted Coconut Layer Cake

After assembling the cake (or any variation), any time before serving, whip 1½ cups heavy cream with 1 tablespoon sugar until almost stiff. Frost the cake with the cream. Cover the top and sides of the cake with 1 cup (1.5 ounces) unsweetened coconut chips, pressing the coconut into the cream. Refrigerate the cake under a bowl or in a covered container until serving.

BERRIES AND CREAM CAKE

The play of tangy fresh berries and sweet preserves with cake and cream is an easy home run here. Pick berries and preserves to match, such as raspberries with raspberry jam, or coordinate raspberries with peach or nectarine jam. You get the idea.

Serves 8 to 10

INGREDIENTS

One-Bowl Vanilla Cake (page 222), baked and cooled

¼ cup to ⅓ cup berry or other fruit jam or preserves

Unsweetened Whipped Cream (page 130)

1½ pints raspberries, blackberries, or other bush berries

Powdered sugar for dusting

DIRECTIONS

Set the cake on a sheet of wax paper. Wrap a length of unflavored dental floss or heavy thread around the "waist" of the cake (if necessary, stick in a few toothpicks to keep the floss centered without shifting), cross the ends of the floss at the front of the cake, and then pull on the ends to cut the cake into 2 even layers. Flip the top layer, cut side up, next to the bottom layer. Spread the bottom layer with preserves. Spread all of the whipped cream over the preserves. Reserving a couple of berries for garnish, arrange the berries over the cream in a single layer, with a little space between them. Press the berries into the cream. Top with the second cake layer, cut side down.

Refrigerate the cake under a bowl or in a covered container for at least 2 hours, or up to a day, to firm the cream and moisten the cake layers.

Remove the cake from the refrigerator 30 minutes before serving. Sift a little powdered sugar over the top of the cake just before serving and garnish with the reserved berries.

✳ VARIATION

Sponge Cake with Berries and Cream

Substitute Nutty Sponge Cake (page 220) or Plain Sponge Cake (page 220) for the vanilla cake. Cut the sponge twice to make three layers and put half of the fillings on each layer.

LEMON LAYER CAKE

This easy layer cake is light and lovely, filled with a whisper of tart lemon curd and clouds of lemon whipped cream.

Serves 10

INGREDIENTS

2 cups heavy cream

2 tablespoons sugar

1 cup chilled Lemon Curd (opposite)

One-Bowl Vanilla Cake (page 222), baked and cooled

Totally Doable Chocolate Shards (page 232) made with white chocolate (optional)

Grated zest of 1 medium lemon (optional)

DIRECTIONS

Whip the cream with the sugar until fairly thick but not quite stiff. Whisk in ½ cup of the lemon curd. Refrigerate.

Set the cake on a sheet of wax paper. Wrap a length of unflavored dental floss or heavy thread around the "waist" of the cake (if necessary, stick in a few toothpicks to keep the floss centered without shifting), cross the ends of the floss at the front of the cake, and then pull on the ends to cut the cake into 2 even layers. Flip the top layer, cut side up, next to the bottom layer.

Spread half of the remaining lemon curd over the cut side of each cake layer. Spread 1½ cups of the lemon whipped cream over the bottom layer. Turn the top layer moist side down on top of the filling. Frost the top and sides of the cake with the remaining lemon whipped cream and cover with broken chocolate shards. Refrigerate the cake for at least 2 hours (longer is better—it keeps for 2 to 3 days) to marry the flavors and moisten the cake layers.

Remove the cake from the refrigerator 30 minutes before serving. For extra fragrance and flavor, if desired, grate a little lemon zest over the cake just before serving.

✳ VARIATION

Blackberry Lemon Layer Cake

Here the cake layers are filled with lemon curd, blackberries, and plain whipped cream, and the cake is left unfrosted.

Reduce the cream to 1 cup and the sugar to 1 tablespoon (or more to taste if the berries are on the tart side). Don't fold any lemon curd into the whipped cream. Spread the lemon curd over the layers as directed. Arrange about 1½ pints blackberries in a single not-too-tight layer over the bottom layer, saving a few for garnish. Spread all of the whipped cream over the berries, pushing it down between them. Top with the second cake layer. Just before serving, sift a little powdered sugar over the cake, and garnish it with the reserved berries.

LEMON CURD

Everyone needs a recipe for lemon curd, and this is the easiest one of all. All of the ingredients go into the pot, and away you go. Don't be afraid of cooking the egg mixture over direct heat: the lemon juice and sugar will prevent the eggs from scrambling even when the mixture starts to simmer. Use the yolkier version if you want egg whites for meringues or pavlova.

Makes 1½ cups

INGREDIENTS

3 large eggs or 1 large egg plus 3 large egg yolks

Grated zest of 1 medium lemon

½ cup strained fresh lemon juice (from about 3 medium lemons)

½ cup (3.5 ounces) sugar

6 tablespoons (3 ounces) unsalted butter, cut into chunks

EQUIPMENT

Medium-fine-mesh strainer

DIRECTIONS

Set the strainer over a medium bowl. Whisk the eggs (or egg and yolks) in a small nonreactive saucepan to blend. Whisk in the lemon zest, juice, and sugar. Add the butter. Whisk over medium heat, reaching into the corners and scraping the sides and bottom of the pan, until the butter is melted and the mixture is thickened and beginning to simmer around the edges, then continue to whisk for about 10 seconds longer. Remove from the heat and scrape into the strainer, pressing gently on the solids. Scrape any lemon curd clinging to the underside of the strainer into the bowl. Refrigerate until chilled before using. Lemon curd keeps in a covered container in the refrigerator for up to 1 week.

TOTALLY DOABLE CHOCOLATE SHARDS

Although they look as though they require a pastry chef's sleight of hand, these curved paper-thin shards of chocolate need only a spatula, some wax paper, and your refrigerator. They keep well and add instant panache to anything from a dish of ice cream to a frosted layer cake.

INGREDIENTS

3 ounces semisweet or bittersweet chocolate, coarsely chopped, or milk or white chocolate, finely chopped (don't use chocolate chips)

DIRECTIONS

Put the chocolate in a medium heatproof bowl, preferably stainless steel. Bring an inch of water almost to a simmer in a wide skillet (see Melting Chocolate My Way, page 97). If using semisweet or bittersweet chocolate, set the bowl directly in the skillet and keep the water at a bare simmer. If using milk or white chocolate, turn the heat off under the skillet and wait for 60 seconds before putting the bowl in the hot water. Stir dark chocolate frequently, milk and white chocolate almost constantly, until almost entirely melted, then remove the bowl, wipe the bottom dry, and stir to finish melting the chocolate.

Tear off two 16-inch-long sheets of wax paper. Scrape the chocolate onto one sheet and use an offset metal spatula or a rubber spatula to spread the chocolate in an even layer, a bit thinner than the cover of a file folder. Cover with the second wax paper sheet and smooth it over the chocolate. Starting at a short end, roll the paper and chocolate up into a 1-inch tube. Refrigerate for at least 2 hours to harden the chocolate completely.

When the chocolate is hard, remove the tube from the fridge and immediately and quickly unroll it, to crack the chocolate into long curved shards. Remove the top sheet of wax paper and turn it clean side up on a tray. Slide a thin metal spatula under the chocolate shards to release them from the wax paper, and slide them onto the tray. Refrigerate until needed.

Shards keep indefinitely, refrigerated in an airtight container. The warmth of your fingers will easily soften or melt the shards, so handle them with a spatula or tongs.

✳ TIP

Even Faster Chocolate Shavings

If you don't want to bother with melting chocolate, just set a bar of chocolate smooth side up on a flat board or tray and rub the surface with the heel of your hand to warm it slightly. Scrape the surface with a sharp paring knife or the sharp edges of a round cookie cutter or a cheese plane. Or shave the edge of the bar with a vegetable peeler after first rubbing the edge with your thumb. Rub the chocolate again if necessary if the shavings get too thin or brittle.

SWEET BITES

Sometimes all that is needed is a little sweet something. Maybe it's a cookie to accompany a bowl of ice cream or a dish of fruit. Or it's sweet spicy nuts, or simple chocolates. Serve these sweet bites as dessert, or after dessert with coffee or dessert wine. Here you'll find bite-sized chocolate truffles; buttery cookies and crunchy amaretti; the easiest way to dip cherries, strawberries, or figs in chocolate; and how to turn a bar of chocolate into a grand dessert.

MINI COOKIE TUTORIAL

Making great cookies is not difficult, but the details really do make the difference. Here is a quick review of what matters.

POSITIONING THE OVEN RACKS

Ovens are hotter on top and in the back. When baking a single sheet of cookies, bake on a rack in the center of the oven and rotate the sheet from front to back halfway through the baking time for even baking. If baking two sheets of cookies, put them in the upper and lower thirds of the oven, and rotate the pans from top to bottom and from back to front for even baking. With a convection oven, you can bake more than two sheets at a time and you may not have to rotate them, if the oven bakes evenly.

PREHEATING THE OVEN

Most ovens need about 15 minutes to reach the set temperature. If your cookies bake much faster or slower than the recipe suggests, check the oven with an oven thermometer set on the center rack and compensate accordingly, or have a professional recalibrate the oven. Everything you bake will come out better at the right temperature!

These recipes were developed and tested in a conventional gas oven, baking no more than two sheets at a time. To bake in a convection oven, follow the instructions in your oven manual: it may tell you to bake at a temperature 25 degrees lower than the recipe calls for and to check for doneness early.

CHOOSING THE RIGHT PANS

Medium- to heavy-weight light-colored aluminum brownie pans and cookie sheets, with or without rims, work better than glass baking pans or light-weight or dark pans, even if they are nonstick. (For more information, see Equipment, page 274.)

LINING BROWNIE PANS

For easy removal and easy cleanup, line brownie pans across the bottom and all the way up two opposite sides with one sheet of foil (quick-release foil is great for this) or parchment paper. Or use my favorite method to line the bottom and all four sides of the pan (it sounds fussy but is actually faster): Tear off a sheet of foil or parchment 4 inches wider and longer than the bottom of the pan. Turn the pan upside down, center the liner on it, and fold the overhang over the sides of the pan. Fold and crease the corners, as though wrapping a present, and slip the liner off the pan. Turn the pan right side up and insert the liner. To remove brownies or bars from the pan, simply lift the edges of the foil or parchment.

LINING COOKIE SHEETS

Pan liners are convenient because they rarely need greasing, they can be "preloaded" while the cookie sheets are in the oven with the first batch, and you can slide them off the pan and onto a rack for cooling (or set the lined pan itself on a rack to cool, since the cookies won't stick to it), rather than removing hot cookies one by one from the hot pan. Parchment paper is the single best all-purpose pan liner. Cookies don't stick to it, and its slight insulating effect promotes even baking and prevents chocolaty batters and meringues from scorching. Precut sheets of parchment (see Resources, page 277) are easier to use (and reuse) than the rolls of paper that come in a box, because the precut sheets will lie flat on the pan instead of curling up. Recipes for certain cookies may call for foil as a first choice and parchment as a second choice because foil produces extra-crispy edges and more caramelization.

If a recipe calls for greased cookie sheets, use a brush or a wad of paper towels to coat them lightly but thoroughly with flavorless vegetable oil or melted butter. Or spray them with vegetable oil spray.

MEASURING FLOUR CORRECTLY

Too much flour is a prime suspect when cookies come out more like paperweights than pleasing pastries. See Measuring, page 172, for information on measuring flour with a scale or a measuring cup.

MIXING COOKIE DOUGH

Too much mixing after the flour is added can produce tough, dry cookies. The recipes will tell you what kind of utensil to mix with, whether to stir or beat, and for how long.

PORTIONING COOKIES

Cookies bake more evenly if they are all the same size. Here are three ways to get there:

- Form a log of any butter cookie dough and chill, then slice and bake.
- Use a cookie scoop (they come in several sizes) with a squeeze-release handle.
- Use a scale to produce equal-sized lumps of dough.

HOW TO FORM A LOG OF COOKIE DOUGH (FOR SLICE-AND-BAKE COOKIES)

Lay an 18-inch length of wax paper horizontally on the counter. Form a rough log 2 or 3 inches shorter than the recipe calls for lengthwise down the center of the paper. If the dough is soft or gooey, just scrape it into a long, uneven shape. Pull the top edge of the paper over the log to cover it. Hold the edge of a ruler (or a straightedge) against the log, pressing against the counter. With your other hand, grip the bottom layer of the paper while pushing the ruler away from you to squeeze and lengthen the log. When the log is the desired length, roll it up in the paper, twist the ends, and refrigerate until chilled.

USING A TIMER

Set the timer for the lesser time first—it's easy to add a minute or two, impossible to subtract. Actually, I set my timer for half of the shortest time so that I don't forget to rotate the cookie sheets.

COOLING COOKIES

Cooling racks allow air to get beneath the item being cooled. You can slide liners from the hot cookie sheets onto a cooling rack, or set the cookie sheets on the rack to cool. If cookies are not baked on liners, transfer each cookie from the pan to the rack. Cookies should be cooled completely before they are wrapped or enclosed in any container for storage, or the moisture trapped in the package may cause mold.

RIGHT-BRAIN NUTTY BUTTER COOKIES

Now, this is a cookie for cooks! I'm an advocate of precise measuring when it comes to baking, but when I find a recipe that is very forgiving and very delicious I'm excited, because it means that even a cook who measures casually will produce a good result and someone who other-wise avoids baking might take a chance. The nuts in these cookies turn out to be the magic ingredient that makes the recipe so forgiving—all those nuts make the cookies both flavorful and tender. And you can have your way with them: choose nuts that are raw or toasted, or even roasted and salted, if you love that salty-sweet effect. Leave them coarsely chopped, or grind them fine for an even more exquisitely tender, melt-in-your-mouth result. The sugar is flexible too—how sweet do you want your cookies? Each decision produces a different result and all are good. (Photograph on page 234)

Makes 4 to 5 dozen cookies

INGREDIENTS

1 to 1½ cups (or a heaping cup) nuts (raw or toasted, or even roasted and salted)

1 very slightly rounded cup (about 5.5 ounces) unbleached all-purpose flour (or half all-purpose and half whole wheat flour)

½ to ⅔ cup (3.5 to 4.625 ounces) sugar

A generous ¼ teaspoon salt (unless you're using salted nuts)

8 tablespoons (4 ounces) unsalted butter, cut into chunks and softened

1 to 2 teaspoons pure vanilla extract

EQUIPMENT

Food processor

Cookie sheets

✳ **TIP**

Good cookies to start with, these get significantly better in flavor, texture, and tenderness if you make the dough 1 to 3 days before you bake (this hydrates the flour and makes everything better) and bake them at least a day before serving.

✳ **VARIATION**

Coconut Cookies

Substitute up to 1 cup of unsweetened shredded dried coconut for the nuts and use a level cup of flour. The dough may seem a bit dry or crumbly when you slice it. Just carry on! Bake the cookies at 325°F and for a little longer, until they are golden brown all over.

DIRECTIONS

FOR COOKIES WITH CHOPPED NUTS Pulse the nuts in the food processor until they are a little coarser than you want them to be. Dump them out and set them aside. Combine the flour, sugar, and salt in the processor and pulse to mix thoroughly. Add the butter and vanilla and process until the mixture is blended, with no visible flour. Add the nuts and pulse just until they are dispersed in the dough.

FOR EXTRA-TENDER COOKIES WITH GROUND NUTS Combine the nuts, flour, sugar, and salt in the food processor and pulse until the nuts are finely ground. Add the butter and vanilla and process until the mixture forms a dough with no visible dry ingredients.

In either case, shape the dough into a 10- to 14-inch-long log (about 1¾ inches in diameter) on a large sheet of wax or parchment paper (or make 2 skinnier logs if you want smaller cookies). Chill for at least 2 hours, until firm enough to slice, or, preferably, overnight; the dough can be refrigerated for up to 3 days.

Position the racks in the upper and lower thirds of the oven and preheat the oven to 350°F. Line the cookie sheets with parchment paper.

Remove the log from the fridge. If the dough is too hard to cut without crumbling, wait for 10 to 20 minutes, until it is still firm but sliceable. Use a sharp knife to cut the log into ¼-inch-thick slices and place them 1½ inches apart on the lined cookie sheets.

Bake for 12 to 14 minutes, until light golden brown at the edges; rotate the sheets from top to bottom and from front to back halfway through the baking time to ensure even baking. Set the pans on racks to cool completely, or slide the parchment liners onto racks. The cookies keep in an airtight container for at least 1 month.

✳ MORE VARIATIONS
6 Ways to Customize Right-Brain Nutty Buttter Cookies

1] Substitute whole wheat pastry flour for all or part of the all-purpose flour.

2] Use brown sugar instead of white sugar.

3] Add about ½ cup raisins or currants or chopped dried fruit.

4] Add a generous tablespoon of brandy, rum, or bourbon along with the vanilla.

5] Add 2 teaspoons ground coffee beans.

6] Replace ⅓ cup of the nuts with roasted cacao nibs, or simply add the nibs without reducing the nuts.

✳ GOOD TO KNOW

A rich, crunchy, nutty butter cookie is the perfect complement to countless fruit or ice cream desserts, or even a simple cup of coffee or tea. You've got instant dessert if you keep them on hand.

AMARETTI

These crunchy flourless almond cookies—quite different from the Right-Brain Nutty Butter Cookies on page 238—elevate even the simplest dish of fruit, bowl of ice cream, or pudding from "regular" to fancy. Serve them with Winter Cherry Compote (page 146) or with Plums in Brandied Coffee Syrup (page 84). They are perfect for dunking in coffee or dessert wine. You can add or substitute hazelnuts, peanuts, walnuts, or pecans (see the variations). Amaretti are easy to make, and they are the basis for endless instantly improvised desserts—see page 242. Amaretti will keep for ages in an airtight container, so they are always there when you need them. And this recipe makes plenty.

Makes about ninety 1½-inch cookies

INGREDIENTS

1⅔ cups (8 ounces) blanched whole almonds

2 cups (8 ounces) powdered sugar

⅛ teaspoon salt

½ cup egg whites (from about 4 large eggs), at room temperature

¼ teaspoon cream of tartar

2 teaspoons pure almond extract

½ cup (3.5 ounces) granulated sugar

EQUIPMENT

Cookie sheets

Food processor

Electric mixer

DIRECTIONS

Position the racks in the upper and lower thirds of the oven and preheat the oven to 300°F. Line the cookie sheets with parchment paper.

Continued

Not properly amaretti, since they contain no almonds, they are nonetheless completely delicious.

Hazelnut or Peanut "Amaretti"

Substitute 1⅔ cups (8 ounces) hazelnuts or 1⅔ cups (6.66 ounces) unsalted, unroasted peanuts for the almonds. Substitute 1½ teaspoons pure vanilla extract for the almond extract.

Walnut or Pecan "Amaretti"

Pecans and walnuts produce a slightly chewy rather than totally crunchy cookie. Substitute 2 cups (7 ounces) walnuts or pecans for the almonds. Substitute 1½ teaspoons pure vanilla extract for the almond extract.

Combine the almonds, powdered sugar, and salt in the food processor and pulse until the nuts are finely ground, scraping the sides as necessary.

Using the electric mixer, beat the egg whites with the cream of tartar in a large clean, dry bowl at medium speed until the egg whites are creamy white and soft peaks are formed when the beaters are lifted. Add the almond extract, then gradually add the granulated sugar, beating until the whites are fluffy and very stiff. Pour the almond mixture over the meringue and fold in with a large rubber spatula just until fully incorporated.

Scoop tablespoons of batter 1 inch apart onto the lined cookie sheets. (While the first two sheets are baking, scoop the remaining batter onto a third lined sheet or onto a parchment liner to be baked when the first batch is done.)

Bake for 30 to 35 minutes, until the cookies are golden; rotate the sheets from top to bottom and from front to back halfway through the baking time to ensure even baking. Set the pans on racks to cool completely, or slide the parchment liners from the pans onto racks. The cookies keep in an airtight container for weeks.

✳ VARIATION

Dessert in a Glass

Use your imagination and taste buds here to create spectacular individual desserts in any glass, including wineglasses or brandy snifters.

Dip amaretti in espresso or strong coffee (with or without brandy or rum), dessert wine, liqueurs, or spirits. Layer dunked cookies (whole or broken) with ricotta or whipped cream, Greek or drained yogurt, crème fraîche, mascarpone, or pastry cream (see page 149). If desired, add any of the following to the layers: chopped candied citrus peel, chopped or shaved chocolate, pistachios or walnuts or toasted almonds, berries or sliced stone fruit or bananas. Serve immediately or chill for a couple of hours to moisten all of the ingredients and blend the flavors.

ULTRATHIN CHOCOLATE CHUNK COOKIES

Hold them up, and you can see through these giant, super-thin (but sturdy!), über-crunchy cookies, bursting with caramel–brown sugar flavor and chunks of bittersweet chocolate. I could not leave this—a blockbuster recipe from *Chewy Gooey Crispy Crunchy Melt-in-Your-Mouth Cookies*—out, or even alone (see page 245 for a sister cookie made with cocoa). One cookie is a dessert unto itself. For the most flavorful cookies, make the dough at least a day ahead.

Makes fifteen 5-inch cookies

INGREDIENTS

1⅓ cups (6 ounces) unbleached all-purpose flour

½ teaspoon baking soda

½ teaspoon salt

10 tablespoons (5 ounces) unsalted butter, melted

½ cup (1.5 ounces) quick-cooking oats

½ cup (3.5 ounces) granulated sugar

¼ cup (1.75 ounces) firmly packed dark brown sugar

2 tablespoons plus 1 teaspoon light corn syrup

2 tablespoons whole milk

1 cup (3.5 ounces) chopped pecans or walnuts (optional)

1 cup (6 ounces) bittersweet or semisweet chocolate chips or chunks

EQUIPMENT

Cookie sheets

DIRECTIONS

Position the racks in the upper and lower thirds of the oven and preheat the oven to 325°F. Line two cookie sheets with foil, dull side up, or parchment paper.

Continued

Combine the flour, baking soda, and salt in a medium bowl and mix together thoroughly with a whisk.

Whisk together the melted butter, oats, sugars, corn syrup, and milk in a large bowl. Mix in the flour mixture. Mix in the nuts, if using. If the dough is warm from the butter, let it cool before adding the chocolate. Stir in the chocolate chips or chunks. (If possible, let the dough rest for at least several hours at room temperature, or, better still, overnight in the fridge. The rest makes for an especially crisp and flavorful cookie.)

Divide the dough into 15 equal portions (each a scant ¼ cup, or about 1.75 ounces). Arrange 5 pieces of dough (4 to make a square and 1 in the center) well apart on each of the lined cookie sheets, keeping in mind that the cookies will spread to 5 inches. With the heel of your hand, flatten each piece of dough until it is about 3½ inches in diameter. Flatten the remaining 5 pieces of dough on another large sheet of foil; set aside.

Bake the two sheets for 18 to 24 minutes, until the cookies are thin and very brown—if they are too pale, they will not be crisp. Rotate the sheets from top to bottom and from front to back halfway through the baking time to ensure even baking. (If the cookies are not baked enough, they will not be perfectly crispy when they are cool. If this happens, you can return the cooled cookies to the oven for a few minutes.)

Slide the sheets of foil onto racks to cool completely before removing the cookies. Bake the third batch; you can even slide the sheet of foil and cookies onto a hot cookie sheet, as long as you immediately put the pan in the oven. The cookies keep in an airtight container for at least 3 days.

ULTRATHIN COCOA PECAN COOKIES

Big ultrathin, ultracrispy cocoa cookies, with a hint of butterscotch flavor and lots of toasty nuts. If you are game, a last-minute sprinkling of freshly grated nutmeg takes the cocoa flavor to new heights.

Makes sixteen 4-inch cookies

INGREDIENTS

1⅓ cups (6 ounces) unbleached all-purpose flour

3 tablespoons unsweetened cocoa powder, preferably natural

½ teaspoon baking soda

Generous ½ teaspoon salt

10 tablespoons (5 ounces) unsalted butter, melted and cooled

⅓ cup (2.33 ounces) firmly packed light brown sugar

⅓ cup (2.33 ounces) granulated sugar

2 tablespoons plus 2 teaspoons light corn syrup

2 tablespoons whole milk

1 teaspoon pure vanilla extract

1 cup (4 ounces) chopped pecans or walnuts

A whole nutmeg (optional)

EQUIPMENT

Cookie sheets

Microplane zester or nutmeg grater (optional)

DIRECTIONS

Mix the flour, cocoa, baking soda, and salt together thoroughly in a medium bowl. Set aside.

Continued

Whisk together the butter, sugars, corn syrup, milk, and vanilla in a large bowl. Stir in the flour mixture. Stir in the nuts. Cover and chill the dough until it is firm enough to scoop, a couple of hours. (If possible, refrigerate overnight; the rest makes for an especially crisp and flavorful cookie.)

Position the racks in the upper and lower thirds of the oven and preheat the oven to 325°F. Line two cookie sheets with parchment paper.

Divide the dough into 16 equal portions (about 2 tablespoons, or 1.4 ounces, each). Arrange 6 pieces of dough well apart on each of the lined cookie sheets, keeping in mind that the cookies will spread to 4 inches as they bake. With the heel of your hand, flatten each piece of dough until it is 3 inches in diameter. Flatten the remaining 4 pieces of dough on another sheet of parchment; set aside.

Bake the two sheets for 15 to 18 minutes, until the cookies are very thin, evenly colored all over, and just beginning to darken very slightly at the edges; rotate the sheets from top to bottom and from front to back halfway through the baking time to ensure even baking. (If the cookies are not baked enough, they will not be perfectly crispy when they are cool. If this happens, you can return the cooled cookies to the oven for a few minutes.)

Slide the parchment liners onto racks to cool completely, or just set the sheets on racks to cool. Bake the third batch; you can even slide the parchment liners and cookies onto a hot cookie sheet, as long as you immediately put the cookie sheet in the oven. The cookies keep in an airtight container for at least 5 days.

Grate a little nutmeg onto the cookies just before serving, if you like.

✳ **VARIATION**

Ultrathin Cocoa Pecan Cookies with Chocolate

Melt 3 ounces semisweet or bittersweet chocolate and drizzle a little over each cooled cookie. Let the chocolate set before storing the cookies layered between sheets of wax paper in an airtight container.

BITTERSWEET BROWNIE DROPS

Here's an easy chocolate cookie with chunks of any kind of chocolate you like, from white to milk to dark. Purchased chocolate chips are more convenient, but hand-chopped chocolate is meltier and more luxurious. For properly moist, slightly gooey cookies, take the cookies out of the oven when they still seem a little soft to the touch; they will firm up as they cool.

Makes about 30 cookies

INGREDIENTS

4 tablespoons (2 ounces) unsalted butter, cut into chunks

8 ounces bittersweet chocolate (70% to 72% cacao), coarsely chopped

⅓ cup plus 1 tablespoon (1.785 ounces) unbleached all-purpose flour

⅛ teaspoon baking soda

Scant 1 cup (6.5 ounces) sugar

¼ teaspoon salt

½ teaspoon pure vanilla extract

2 large eggs

1 cup (3.5 ounces) walnut or pecan pieces (I like walnuts untoasted but generally toast pecans)

6 ounces bittersweet, semisweet, milk, or white chocolate, coarsely chopped, or 1 cup (6 ounces) chocolate chips

EQUIPMENT

Cookie sheets

DIRECTIONS

Position the racks in the upper and lower thirds of the oven and preheat the oven to 350°F. Line the cookie sheets with parchment paper.

Continued

Put the butter and bittersweet chocolate in a medium heatproof bowl, preferably stainless steel, set it in a wide skillet of barely simmering water (see Melting Chocolate My Way, page 97), and stir frequently until the mixture is melted, smooth, and fairly hot to the touch.

Meanwhile, whisk the flour and baking soda together thoroughly in a small bowl.

When the chocolate mixture is ready, remove the bowl from the water bath and stir in the sugar, salt, and vanilla. Add the eggs one at a time, stirring until incorporated. Add the flour mixture and stir vigorously with a wooden spoon or a rubber spatula until the batter is smooth and glossy and comes away from the sides of the bowl; it is critical that the batter pull itself together, so don't stop mixing until it does. Make sure that the batter is completely cool, then stir in the nuts and chopped chocolate or chips.

Scoop slightly rounded tablespoons of the batter and place 2 inches apart onto the lined cookie sheets. Bake for 10 to 12 minutes, until the cookies are puffed and crackled on the surface but feel slightly soft when you touch them with a fingertip; rotate the sheets from top to bottom and from front to back halfway through the baking time to ensure even baking. Set the sheets on racks to cool completely, or slide the parchment liners onto racks. The cookies keep in an airtight container for 2 to 3 days.

COCOA BROWNIES
WITH WALNUTS AND BROWN BUTTER

Deeply chocolate walnut-laced brownies with the fragrant flavor of browned butter. The batter is thick enough to spread with deep swirls, and the result is soft, gooey brownies with slightly crusty tops. These brownies are thin, and I like them that way.

Makes 16 large or 25 small brownies

INGREDIENTS

10 tablespoons (5 ounces) unsalted butter, cut into 1-inch chunks

1¼ cups (8.75 ounces) sugar

¾ cup (2.4 ounces) unsweetened cocoa powder, preferably natural

Rounded ¼ teaspoon salt

2 teaspoons water

1 teaspoon pure vanilla extract

2 cold large eggs

⅓ cup plus 1 tablespoon (1.78 ounces) unbleached all-purpose flour

1 cup (3.5 ounces) walnut pieces

EQUIPMENT

8-inch square baking pan

DIRECTIONS

Position a rack in the lower third of the oven and preheat the oven to 325°F. Line the bottom and all 4 sides of the baking pan with foil (see page 236) and coat with nonstick vegetable spray (or use nonstick foil).

Continued

✳ **GOOD TO KNOW**

I think the taste of brown butter goes especially well with natural rather than Dutch-process cocoa, and I particularly recommend Scharffen Berger natural cocoa. If you need to make two batches of brownies, use natural cocoa in one and Dutch-process in the other. Your guests will enjoy seeing and tasting the difference, and everyone will have a preference.

Melt the butter in a medium saucepan and continue to cook, whisking gently, until it is golden brown and the milk particles suspended in it are reddish brown. Remove the pan from the heat and stop the cooking by immediately adding the sugar, cocoa powder, salt, water, and vanilla. Stir to blend. Let cool for 5 minutes; the mixture will still be fairly hot.

Add the eggs one at a time, beating vigorously with a wooden spoon or a silicone spatula after adding each one. When the mixture looks thick, shiny, and well blended, add all of the flour and stir until you no longer see streaks of flour, then beat vigorously for 50 to 60 strokes with the wooden spoon or the spatula. Stir in the nuts.

Spread the batter in the lined pan, swirling the surface if you like. Bake for 20 to 25 minutes, until a toothpick inserted in the center comes out almost clean (the brownies will still be soft and gooey even if the toothpick looks clean). Cool the brownies in the pan on a rack.

Lift the edges of the foil liner and transfer the brownies to a cutting board. Slide a metal spatula under the brownies to detach them from the foil (or invert the brownies and peel off the foil, then turn the brownies right side up again). Cut into 16 or 25 squares. The brownies keep stored airtight for 2 to 3 days.

GRILLED CHOCOLATE SANDWICHES

Crusty, hot, and melty chocolate sandwiches make a decadent snack, but cut into daintier portions and nestled with a scoop of vanilla ice cream, they make a dynamite dessert for company. They're fun too.

Makes 2 sandwiches

INGREDIENTS

Unsalted butter

4 slices sweet or sourdough French bread or firm white sandwich bread

About 2 ounces broken or chopped semisweet or bittersweet chocolate, or ⅓ cup chocolate chips

Coarse sea salt (optional)

1 tablespoon sugar mixed with ⅛ teaspoon ground cinnamon (optional)

DIRECTIONS

Butter one side of each slice of bread generously. In a skillet big enough to hold them, cook the slices butter side down over medium heat, just until pale gold on one side. Cover two of the slices with chocolate. Flip a naked slice on top, butter side up. Cook, turning the sandwiches as necessary, until the chocolate is softened and the sandwiches are browned on both sides. Serve immediately, sprinkled with a pinch of sea salt or a dusting of cinnamon sugar, if you like.

GOING NUTS: HOW TO BUY, STORE, TOAST, AND GRIND THEM

BUYING AND STORING NUTS

For freshness and flavor, buy nuts raw, rather than toasted, and preferably from busy stores that sell them in bulk. Whole almonds, hazelnuts, or peanuts and halves or large pieces of walnuts and pecans stay fresher longer; it's better to chop nuts yourself. And it's best to toast whole nuts or large pieces before chopping or pulverizing them. Unless you blast through nuts quickly, keep your supply in the freezer, packaged airtight.

THE BEST WAY TO TOAST NUTS

Nuts are delicious raw, but toasting brings out such rich flavors that almonds and hazelnuts are virtually transformed. Toasted nuts are also extra crunchy. Toast the nuts in a single layer on a baking sheet and bake in a preheated oven (350°F for almonds and hazelnuts, 325°F for pecans and walnuts) for 10 to 20 minutes, depending on the type of nut and whether they are whole, sliced, or slivered. Check the nuts frequently and redistribute them on the pan. Almonds and hazelnuts are done when they are golden brown inside. Pecans and walnuts are done when they are fragrant and lightly colored.

To rub the skins from toasted hazelnuts, cool them thoroughly, then rub them together in your hands or in a tea towel, or place them in a large coarse-mesh strainer and rub them against the mesh until most of the skins flake off.

THE BEST WAY TO PULVERIZE NUTS

To pulverize nuts in a food processor without turning them into paste, start with a dry bowl and blade at room temperature (not hot from the dishwasher). The nuts should also be at room temperature: frozen or cold nuts will give off moisture that will turn them to paste, as will toasted nuts still hot from the oven. Scrape the sides of the processor bowl with a chopstick or a rubber spatula from time to time. If you observe these rules, there will be no need to add flour or sugar from the recipe to the nuts to keep them dry, as many cookbooks advise, although that can be a good precaution.

SPICED AND CANDIED NUTS

These sweet crunchy bites range from just plain delicious to unusual and exotic *and* just plain delicious. Whether you serve them with coffee or cocktails, or incorporate them into another dessert, you'll find them easy to make and endlessly useful.

BOURBON–BROWN SUGAR PECANS

These taste like gingerbread pralines. They're a perfect topper for ice cream and caramel sauce.

Makes about 3 cups

1 cup (7 ounces) firmly packed brown sugar

¼ cup bourbon

4 tablespoons (2 ounces) unsalted butter

½ teaspoon salt

3 cups (10.5 ounces) raw pecan halves

½ teaspoon ground cinnamon

1 teaspoon ground ginger

¼ teaspoon ground cloves

Line a baking sheet with parchment paper. Combine the sugar, bourbon, butter, salt, and pecans in a large skillet and cook over medium-high heat, stirring with a silicone spatula or a wooden spoon, until the sugar melts and gets darker and the pecans smell toasted, 5 to 6 minutes. Remove the pan from the heat, stir in the spices, and mix thoroughly.

Scrape the hot mixture onto the parchment-lined pan, spread the nuts out, and let cool.

Break the nut mixture into pieces. The nuts are most delicious in the first 2 weeks or so. Store in an airtight container or a zip-lock freezer bag to prevent them from getting sticky.

CANDIED COCONUT-CARDAMOM CASHEWS

These are fabulous. Serve them with a platter of tropical fruit or fruit salad, or with mango sorbet.

Makes about 3 cups

1 cup (7 ounces) firmly packed brown sugar

1 cup (7 ounces) granulated sugar

¼ cup water

2 teaspoons pure vanilla extract

½ teaspoon salt

2 cups (3 ounces) unsweetened large-flake dried coconut

3 cups (10.5 ounces) unsalted toasted cashews

1 teaspoon cardamom seeds (from 16 to 20 pods)

Line a baking sheet with parchment paper. Combine the sugars, water, vanilla, salt, and coconut in a large skillet and cook over medium-high heat, stirring with a silicone spatula or a wooden spoon, until the sugars melt and get darker and the coconut looks and smells toasted, 3 to 4 minutes. Remove the pan from the heat, stir in the nuts and cardamom, and mix thoroughly.

Scrape the hot mixture onto the parchment-lined pan, spread the nuts out, and let cool.

Break the nut mixture into pieces. The nuts are most delicious in the first 2 weeks or so. Store in an airtight container or a zip-lock freezer bag to prevent them from getting sticky.

ORANGE-GLAZED WALNUTS WITH CACAO NIBS

The cacao nibs make these crunchy and satisfyingly bitter. Sprinkle them over a dollop of whipped cream atop a dish of chocolate pudding to add character and crunch.

Makes about 3 cups

½ cup (3.5 ounces) firmly packed brown sugar

1 cup (7 ounces) granulated sugar

2 tablespoons fresh orange juice

1 teaspoon pure vanilla extract

¼ teaspoon salt

3 cups (10.5 ounces) raw walnuts

1 teaspoon grated orange zest

1 cup (4 ounces) roasted cacao nibs

Line a baking sheet with parchment paper. Combine the sugars, orange juice, vanilla, salt, and nuts in a large skillet and cook over medium-high heat, stirring with a silicone spatula or a wooden spoon, until the sugars melt and get darker and the walnuts smell toasted, 5 to 6 minutes. Remove the pan from the heat, stir in the zest and nibs, and mix thoroughly.

Scrape the hot mixture onto the parchment-lined pan, spread the nuts out, and let cool.

Break the nut mixture into pieces. The nuts are most delicious in the first 2 weeks or so. Store in an airtight container or a zip-lock freezer bag to prevent them from getting sticky.

HONEY PISTACHIOS WITH FENNEL

Subtler than the other spiced and candied nuts, these are luxurious and a must for fennel fans.

Makes about 3 cups

½ cup (3.5 ounces) firmly packed brown sugar

½ cup (3.5 ounces) granulated sugar

¼ cup honey

¼ teaspoon salt

3 cups (10.5 ounces) raw pistachio nuts

1 tablespoon fennel seeds

Line a baking sheet with parchment paper. Combine the sugars, honey, salt, and nuts in a large skillet and cook over medium-high heat, stirring with a silicone spatula or a wooden spoon, until the sugars melt and get darker and the pistachios smell toasted, 3 to 4 minutes. Remove the pan from the heat, stir in the fennel, and mix thoroughly.

Scrape the hot mixture onto the parchment-lined pan, spread the nuts out, and let cool.

Break the nut mixture into pieces. The nuts are most delicious in the first 2 weeks or so. Store in an airtight container or a zip-lock freezer bag to prevent them from getting sticky.

CHEESE AND HONEY

This simple dessert, known as *mel i mato* in Catalonia, is served at Bar César in my Berkeley neighborhood.

Arrange toasted nuts and pieces of dried fruit around a serving of fresh fromage blanc, mild creamy goat cheese, yogurt cheese (page 114), or ricotta. Drizzle with honey. Serve with a dessert wine.

MORE IDEAS FOR CHEESE

- Serve a good cheddar with sliced apples and honey.

- Serve an English Stilton (or French Roquefort or American blue . . .) cheese with walnuts and port.

- Serve Gorgonzola dolcelatte with chestnut honey (or another dark, flavorful honey).

- Serve fromage blanc generously sprinkled with sugar and surrounded by strawberries.

- Serve warm Brie (baked in a 325° oven until soft and gooey inside) with any seasonal fruit and plain crackers.

8 IDEAS FOR A BAR OF CHOCOLATE

At my house, we taste a lot of chocolate in an informal and spontaneous way. We sit at the table with a bar or two or three of some new or interesting chocolate, or a familiar one that we love, on a wooden cutting board. I break the bars into small pieces with the tip of a sharp paring knife. We nibble. The ritual becomes more elaborate, and more like dessert than a "tasting," if I add toasted nuts, fresh or dried fruit, even a fresh or hard cheese. It is fascinating to see how different chocolates pair with the various ingredients. Think of it as you might a cheese course, but different! Serve a little dessert wine or the rich red wine left from dinner. Here are some other ways to turn a bar of chocolate into a dessert.

1] Make classic s'mores with graham crackers and marshmallows. Or substitute buttered and toasted baguette slices or Spice-Drawer Cinnamon Toast (page 28) for the graham crackers.

2] Make a rich chocolate demitasse: For 3 servings, put 3 ounces semisweet or bittersweet chocolate, finely chopped, in a small saucepan, pour ⅓ cup boiling water over it, and stir until the chocolate is melted and smooth. Stir in another ⅓ cup boiling water, followed by ⅔ cup whole milk. Heat gently, whisking or stirring, until the chocolate is steaming hot but not simmering. Serve immediately, with cookies or Spice-Drawer Cinnamon Toast (page 28). You can offer ground cinnamon, cardamom, ancho chile, black pepper, or other spices for guests to sprinkle (just a pinch or so) over the chocolate to taste.

3] Grill slices of fresh pineapple and pile them on a platter, interspersed with chopped chocolate.

4] Top Spice-Drawer Cinnamon Toast (page 28) with small chunks of chocolate and let them melt.

5] Finely chop chocolate and stir into sweetened ricotta along with chopped candied orange peel and pistachios or toasted almonds.

6] Strew chopped chocolate over a hot buttered corn tortilla, sprinkle with ground cinnamon or cardamom and sugar and/or chopped nuts, fold, and serve.

7] Split a baguette in half, butter generously, and stuff with pieces of chocolate.

8] Make a chocolate pizzetta: bake purchased pizza dough as directed and top in the last 5 minutes with chunks of chocolate and cinnamon sugar.

CHOCOLATE-DIPPED FRUIT

You can buy expensive chocolate-covered fruit, or you can make it yourself, with better chocolate and fruit that you know is ripe and flavorful. Choose a brand of chocolate that you love to nibble. (And choose a bar of chocolate rather than chocolate chips or anything called "chocolate coating," even if it is sold in the same aisle as the fruit. Chocolate chips won't melt well, and the chocolate coating is not delicious enough.) No need to "temper" the chocolate to keep it shiny: the secret to preventing the chocolate from turning gray and streaky is to dry and chill the fruit before dipping, then refrigerate it as soon after dipping as possible.

Serves 15 or more

INGREDIENTS

About 2 pints small or medium strawberries (with or without stems), or up to 36 large strawberries with stems or figs, or 1¼ pounds cherries with stems

8 ounces bittersweet or semisweet chocolate, coarsely chopped, or milk or white chocolate, finely chopped

EQUIPMENT

Cookie sheets

Fluted paper candy cups (optional)

DIRECTIONS

Rinse the fruit gently and spread it out on a tray lined with paper towels. The fruit should be as dry as possible before dipping; if necessary, pat it dry or use a cupped hand to cradle each piece gently in a soft dish towel or a paper towel. Refrigerate until chilled.

Line the cookie sheets with parchment paper.

Put the chocolate in a small heatproof bowl, preferably stainless steel. Bring an inch of water to a simmer in a wide skillet (see Melting Chocolate My Way, page 97). If using semisweet or bittersweet chocolate, set the bowl directly in the skillet and keep the water at a bare simmer.

❄ GOOD TO KNOW

If you are dipping cherries, be sure to warn your guests about the pits.

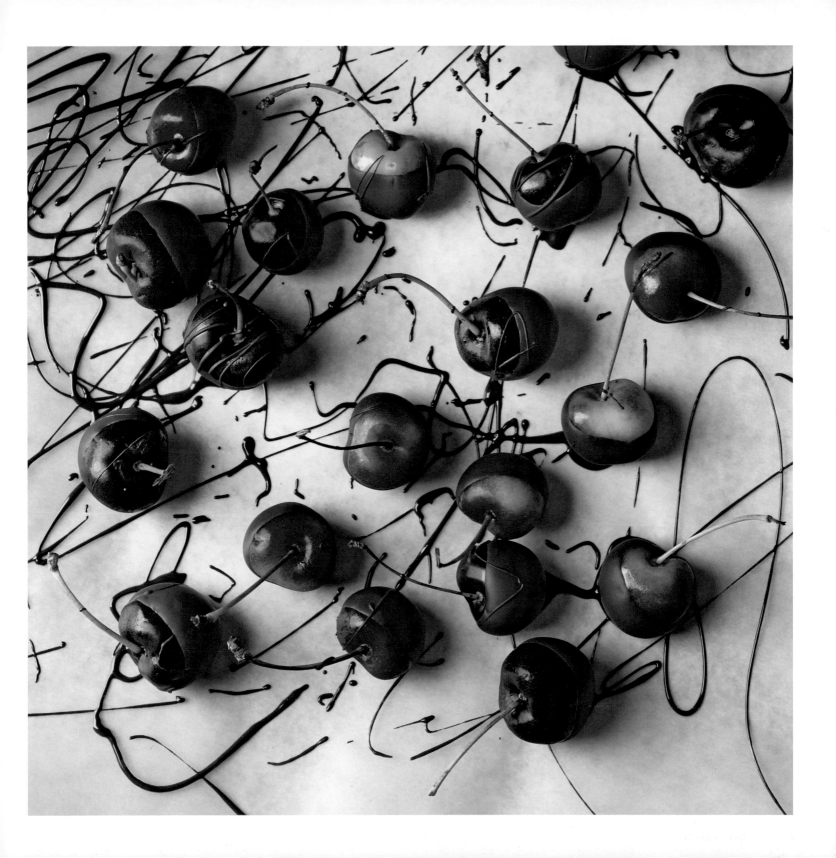

If using milk or white chocolate, turn the heat off under the skillet and wait for 60 seconds before putting the bowl in the hot water. Stir dark chocolate frequently, milk and white chocolate almost constantly, until almost entirely melted, then remove the bowl, wipe the bottom dry, and stir to finish melting the chocolate. (To melt chocolate in the microwave, see page 98.) The chocolate should be warm and fluid, but not hot.

Grasp fruit by the stem or the shoulders and dip it about two-thirds of the way into the chocolate, or deeper if you like. Lift the fruit above the chocolate and shake off the excess, letting it drip back into the bowl, then very gently wipe a little excess chocolate from one side of the fruit on the edge of the bowl, set it on a lined cookie sheet, wiped side down, and slide it forward slightly to prevent a puddle of chocolate from forming at the tip. Refrigerate each tray as soon as it's filled, and keep refrigerated until ready to serve.

Serve any time after the chocolate has set enough that you can peel the fruit cleanly from the parchment. Transfer each one to a fluted candy cup, if desired.

MY HOUSE TRUFFLES 4.0

I started my career making and selling bite-sized, hand-rolled, cocoa-dusted truffles in Berkeley in the early 1970s. The original recipe, from my French landlady, remains a treasure. I have updated it over the years to meet the challenges of food safety (the original recipe was made with raw egg yolks), new and better chocolates, and our changing taste buds. If you've followed me, you may think you already have this recipe once and for all, but I promise that you don't. Today my house truffles have a touch of salt, a vastly easier method of heating the yolks, and a new, ultrasmooth texture. You cannot buy truffles like these. And if you love the idea of chocolate truffles with red wine, these are the most wine-friendly truffles you will ever find.

Makes 64 or more truffles

INGREDIENTS

2 large egg yolks, at room temperature

1 pound bittersweet or semisweet chocolate (no more than 62% cacao), coarsely chopped

10 tablespoons (5 ounces) unsalted butter, cut into small pieces

⅛ teaspoon salt, preferably fine sea salt

⅓ cup (1 ounce) unsweetened cocoa powder, preferably natural, or as needed

EQUIPMENT

Food processor

Fine-mesh strainer

8-inch square baking pan, lined on the bottom and all sides with foil

DIRECTIONS

Put the egg yolks in a small heatproof bowl, preferably stainless steel, and set the bowl in a large container of very hot water to heat the egg yolks until barely lukewarm. Set aside.

Continued

✳ GOOD TO KNOW

Rolling the truffles in cocoa to make them round is the step that takes the longest and makes the biggest mess. But you can skip it! Leave the truffles square. Rather than tossing them in the cocoa with your hands (messy) or with a utensil (which tends to dent them), simply pour them back and forth between two bowls until they are coated. Easy!

Meanwhile, put the chocolate, butter, and salt in a medium heatproof bowl, preferably stainless steel, set it in a wide skillet of barely simmering water (see Melting Chocolate My Way, page 97), and stir frequently until the chocolate and butter are melted and the mixture is smooth and quite warm. (If you have an instant-read thermometer, the temperature should be between 120° and 130°F.) Scrape the mixture into the food processor and set the strainer over the processor bowl.

Bring ½ cup water to a boil in a very small saucepan or in a glass measure in the microwave. Remove the egg yolk bowl from the large container and immediately pour the boiling water steadily into the egg yolks, stirring constantly with a silicone spatula. (When the yolks and water are blended, the temperature should be at least 160°F.) Pour the mixture through the strainer into the food processor. Tap the strainer against the bowl to encourage all of the liquid to flow through, but don't press on or mess with any bits of cooked egg in the strainer. Process the mixture for a few seconds, then scrape the bowl and process again for 20 or 30 seconds, or as long as it takes for the mixture to thicken and resemble satiny-smooth chocolate pudding. Scrape the mixture into the lined pan and spread it evenly. Let cool, then cover and refrigerate until firm, at least a few hours.

TO SHAPE THE TRUFFLES Put half of the cocoa in a small bowl. Remove the baking pan from the refrigerator and use the liner to remove the truffle sheet. Invert it on a cutting board and peel off the liner. Cut the truffles into 1-inch squares (or smaller, if you prefer) and toss them in the cocoa powder, adding more cocoa as necessary. You can leave the truffles square or dust your hands with cocoa and roll them into balls. Shake the truffles gently in a coarse strainer to remove excess cocoa. Store the truffles, tightly covered, in the refrigerator for up to 2 weeks, or in the freezer for up to 3 months.

Remove the truffles from the refrigerator about 15 minutes before serving. Sift a little extra cocoa over them as necessary.

INGREDIENTS

BAKING POWDER AND BAKING SODA

Baking powder has an expiration date, because it loses its oomph if it's not fresh and if it's not stored in a tightly sealed container. To see if baking powder is still good, add about 1 teaspoon to ¼ cup hot water. If it bubbles vigorously, use it. If in doubt, toss out the old container and buy a new one.

Baking soda appears to last indefinitely in the cupboard. If you are unsure, spoon a bit into a cup and add vinegar. If it bubbles vigorously, it's fine.

BUTTER (AND MARGARINE)

The recipes in this book call for unsalted butter, the usual choice of bakers and pastry chefs. If you use salted butter, subtract ¼ teaspoon salt from the quantity in the recipe for each stick (8 tablespoons) of butter. If you must or prefer to use margarine, choose one labeled suitable for baking; some "light" margarine spreads and butter substitutes have too much water for successful baking.

BUTTER, EUROPEAN AND EUROPEAN-STYLE

These butters contain 82 to 87 percent fat, compared with our American standard 80 percent, and thus less water. Some are made from cultured milk, which gives them a nutty or pleasing mild fresh cheese flavor. The flavor of European-style butters varies considerably from brand to brand; some are truly magnificent. If you bake with European-style butter, however, its higher fat and lower moisture content may adversely affect your results: for example, cookies may spread too much on the baking sheet and seem greasy. Using 5 to 10 percent less butter than called for in the recipe sometimes prevents such problems. Or just save the special butter for your morning toast, and bake with regular butter.

CHOCOLATE

Here is a brief glossary of the different types and forms of chocolate used in my recipes. See also How to Choose Bittersweet and Semisweet Chocolates, page 97.

ROASTED CACAO NIBS

Cacao (or cocoa) nibs are pieces of roasted and hulled cocoa beans, the basis of all types of chocolate. Nibs are crunchy and somewhat bitter. Crushed, ground, chopped, or left in their natural form, they add unique chocolate flavor to all kinds of desserts. Raw nibs are available, but I vastly prefer the flavor of roasted nibs. Cocoa nibs are available in better supermarkets or online (see Resources, page 277).

UNSWEETENED CHOCOLATE

Technically called chocolate liquor (though it contains no alcohol), unsweetened chocolate is pure ground cacao nibs, often with a fraction of a percent of lecithin as an emulsifier. (Some unsweetened chocolate may be labeled "99% cacao" to account for that tiny amount of lecithin.) The highest-quality unsweetened chocolate is smooth enough and palatable enough to nibble.

SEMISWEET AND BITTERSWEET CHOCOLATES

Bittersweet and semisweet chocolates are sweetened dark chocolates: pure ground cocoa beans; optional cocoa butter; sugar; optional lecithin and/or vanilla; and sometimes a small amount of milk have been added. The standard brands in the baking aisle contain 50 to 60 percent cacao and thus 40 to 50 percent sugar. But there are dozens of semisweet and bittersweet chocolates with ever higher cacao percentages. And while bittersweet is generally less sweet than semisweet, there is no official distinction between them, so one brand of bittersweet may be sweeter than another brand of semisweet. Cacao percentage is a better predictor of sweetness and chocolate intensity than these less specific terms. See How to Choose Bittersweet and Semisweet Chocolates, page 97.

MILK CHOCOLATE

Milk chocolate is sweetened chocolate that contains at least 10 percent cocoa beans and a minimum of 12 percent milk solids, plus milk fat. The most flavorful milk chocolates exceed the minimum cacao requirement considerably, resulting in chocolate with more chocolate flavor and less sweetness.

WHITE CHOCOLATE

White chocolate is made from only the fat of the cocoa bean (cocoa butter), rather than the whole cocoa bean, combined with sugar, dry milk solids, milk fat, lecithin, and vanilla. White chocolate is now recognized and defined by the FDA as a form of real chocolate and should not be confused with "white confectionery coating," which is made from other tropical vegetable fats and contains not a single ingredient derived from cocoa beans.

CHOCOLATE CHIPS AND CHUNKS

Commercial chocolate chips (and some chocolate chunks) are specially formulated with less cocoa butter than bar chocolate so that they hold their shape when baked into cookies. They may also help keep cookies from flattening out during baking. Since chocolate chips (and chocolate chunks formulated similarly) stay thick when melted and are usually fairly sweet, they are not recommended for melting and blending into batters. You can chop your favorite chocolate bars instead of using commercial chocolate chips or chunks, as long as you don't mind cookies that are a little flatter and chips or chunks that flow a little rather than hold their original shape.

Also see Cocoa Powder Fact Sheet, page 177.

COCONUT

Some of the recipes in this book call for unsweetened shredded dried coconut and/or coconut chips (wide strips of unsweetened shaved dried coconut). Both have superb true coconut flavor in cookies, and neither has preservatives or sugar. Both are found in better supermarkets, in specialty markets that sell nuts and dried fruit in bulk, in natural food and health food stores, and online (see Resources, page 277).

Sweetened coconut, flaked or shredded, is found in the baking aisle of most supermarkets.

COFFEE AND ESPRESSO POWDER

If a recipe calls for freshly ground coffee beans, use freshly roasted beans from a specialty purveyor, and grind the beans yourself if possible. For recipes that call for espresso powder, I prefer Medaglia d'Oro instant espresso powder rather than freeze-dried crystals.

CREAM

The best-tasting cream is simply pasteurized, rather than ultra-pasteurized or sterilized (for longer shelf life), and contains no added ingredients. If you want to have cream on hand for just-in-case, keep a carton of ultra-pasteurized in the back of the fridge (it lasts for a long time unopened). But when you know you are going to make a dessert, buy the good stuff if there is a choice.

DRIED FRUITS

These should be moist, plump, and flavorful. Whole pieces are always better, fresher, and moister than prechopped or extruded pellets.

Use an oiled knife or oiled scissors to cut or chop sticky dried fruit.

EXTRA VIRGIN OLIVE OIL

Extra virgin olive oil is a flavoring ingredient as well as a fat! I use it in desserts for its own good taste rather than as a substitute for butter. Choose fragrant, flavorful oil, and don't hesitate to try different styles, from delicate to robust.

FLOUR

The recipes in this book were tested with a national brand of unbleached all-purpose flour. Bleached flour makes the most tender cookies and cakes because it usually has slightly less protein than unbleached flour, because it is more finely milled, and because the bleaching process acidifies the flour, which also has a tenderizing effect. But unbleached flour is a purer, less processed ingredient and has a better taste.

GINGER

See A Jolt of Ginger, page 212.

NUTS

See Going Nuts: How to Buy, Store, Toast, and Grind Them, page 256.

SPICES

Use ground spices that still smell potent in the jar. Grinding one's own spices may seem extreme to many American cooks, but you can come partway with only minimal effort: whole nutmeg and cinnamon sticks are easy to grate on the spot using a Microplane zester. And it's not that hard to smash the pods and pick the seeds from whole cardamom pods and crush them in a little mortar. The rewards are significant in terms of flavor and aroma.

SUGAR

GRANULATED SUGAR

All of the recipes in this book, with the exception of the pavlova (see page 161), were tested with C&H granulated cane sugar, purchased at the supermarket. I tested the pavlova with C&H bakers' sugar and with regular granulated sugar pulverized in a food processor. Sugar varies in different parts of the country. If your brand of sugar is coarser than regular salt and/or you think that your cakes or cookies could be more tender, switch to C&H bakers' sugar, use superfine or bar sugar, or process your granulated sugar briefly in the food processor before using it. I use pure cane sugar rather than beet sugar for baking and dessert making. Chemically the two substances are

the same, but many bakers and pastry chefs have reported differences and disappointments with beet sugar.

BROWN SUGAR

Originally brown sugar was semirefined, with some of the natural molasses left in (see Raw Sugars, following). Today commercial brown sugar is retrofitted: that is, it is refined white sugar with added molasses. The resulting light (or golden) and dark brown sugars impart pleasing caramel or butterscotch flavors. Some recipes may specify light or dark brown sugar, but usually you can use them interchangeably.

Brown sugar and moist raw sugars harden with exposure to the air; store them in an airtight container or tightly sealed in the bag they came in. The sugar should be lump free before it is added to a batter or a dough, as it is unlikely to smooth out once it is incorporated. Soft lumps can be squeezed with your fingers or mashed with a fork. To soften hardened brown sugar, sprinkle it with a little water, put it in a tightly covered container (or wrap tightly in foil), and place it in a 250°F oven for a few minutes; allow it to cool before using it. Brown sugar is measured by packing it fairly firmly into a measuring cup.

RAW SUGARS

Raw sugars (all of which are actually cooked in processing) are more accurately described as semirefined sugars, with varying amounts of the natural molasses left in them. They range in color and consistency from coarse crystals with a light caramel hue (and flavor to match) to amber, russet, or deep mahogany brown, with the moist consistency of familiar brown sugar. The best of them burst with complex tastes and aromas.

Turbinado, Demerara, and evaporated cane juice sugars are semirefined cane sugars with coarse crystals and delicate caramel-toffee flavors. Often served with coffee or tea, they can also be substituted for a little of the granulated sugar in shortbread and butter cookie doughs, adding flavor, crunch, and tenderness. Or sprinkle them in lieu of granulated sugar on top of anything. Demerara tends to be a little darker and more flavorful than turbinado sugar.

From Barbados or Mauritius, muscovado sugar is a semirefined cane sugar, with lots of the natural molasses left in it. Soft and moist, it has an earthy, ripe-tropical-fruit flavor and aroma, with a touch of smoke. Light muscovado has the intensity and sweetness of regular dark brown sugar (for which it can be substituted), but with far more flavor and complexity. Almost black, dark muscovado has deep aromatic molasses notes.

In Mexican groceries, you will find boiled sugarcane juice molded into cone shapes. Called *piloncillo* (or *panocha* or *panela*), it must be grated or smashed with a hammer in order to be used. Palm or coconut sugar comes, respectively, from sugar palm or coconut palm trees. These sugars are found in Asian markets, usually molded into shapes that must also be grated or smashed, but some health food or whole food markets carry granulated coconut sugar. All of these are flavorful alternatives to ordinary brown sugar.

POWDERED SUGAR

Also called confectioners' sugar or icing sugar, this is granulated sugar that has been pulverized and mixed with a little cornstarch to prevent clumping. I use powdered sugar mostly for dusting, sifting it over cakes to soften or dress up the look.

THAI TEA

Thai tea is a blend of black tea, dried pandan leaves, and lemongrass. Some brands may contain star anise, crushed tamarind seed, and/or other spices as well. Brewed into a strong, sweet tea served over crushed ice with a generous amount of evaporated milk, it has become very popular—even outside of Thai restaurants. Thai tea is available in Asian groceries and online (see Resources, page 277); look for loose tea leaves rather than powder or instant mixes.

VANILLA

See The Virtues of Vanilla, page 53.

EQUIPMENT

Successful dessert making requires only simple basic equipment. Even a cook with a minimally equipped kitchen can turn out great desserts, as long as the oven is reliable and the pans are adequate.

BOWLS

Glass and stainless steel bowls are good for different tasks. Glass bowls work in the microwave, and their weight makes them stable when you must whisk or beat with one hand while pouring in an ingredient with the other. But stainless steel is more versatile, and it is preferable for melting chocolate or heating ingredients in a water bath or an improvised double boiler. Bowls that are nearly as tall as they are wide are the best shape for beating egg whites and for keeping sugar and flour from flying out when using a handheld mixer.

CAKE AND BROWNIE PANS

The recipes in this book use 8- and 9-inch round and square pans, all 2 inches deep; 8- and 9-inch springform pans, 2½ to 3 inches deep; 9-by-13-inch baking pans; 10-inch glass or ceramic pie plates; and 10-inch tube pans with removable bottoms.

For even baking and moist, tender cake layers, medium- to heavy-weight light-colored aluminum cake and brownie pans generally work best. Glass pans and metal pans that are thin or dark tend to produce cakes that overbake at the sides and on the bottom, sometimes even before the inside is done. There are always exceptions: some pound cakes and rich cakes baked in very heavy (often decorative and often dark) tube, Bundt, or loaf pans acquire a deep golden-brown crust that is both delicious and beautiful. Always read the information that comes with these pans; you may be advised to lower the baking temperature by 25 degrees—which is the standard advice when you bake in a glass rather than a metal pan.

COOKIE SCOOPS

Not essential but wonderful, cookie scoops with squeeze-and-release handles are the fast and easy way to make lots of evenly sized drop cookies or balls of dough. Scoops in many different sizes are found at cookware stores and are available by mail order (see Resources, page 277).

COOKIE SHEETS

Medium- to heavy-weight light-colored aluminum pans, with or without rims, work better than lightweight or dark pans, even if they are non-stick. If your oven temperature is accurate but cookies bake unevenly or brown too much or too quickly on the bottom and edges, your pans may be too thin or too dark. Parchment paper liners help promote even baking if your pans are less than ideal.

COOLING RACKS

Whether it's an inexpensive one from the hardware store or a fancy French version, you need some kind of rack so cakes and cookies can cool quickly with lots of air circulation.

FOOD PROCESSOR AND BLENDER

A food processor makes cookie and pie dough and even some cake batters in a flash. It purees fruit for sauce, emulsifies chocolate ganache, and pulverizes nuts. It also enables you to make ice cream without an ice cream maker. Blenders, although they puree and emulsify better than food processors, are less versatile and don't do as good a job pulverizing nuts, often turning them to paste if you are not careful.

MEASURES: DRY AND LIQUID

Dry measures refer to measuring cups designed to measure dry ingredients; they are made of metal or plastic and come in sets. Dry measures are meant to be filled to the rim and leveled. Liquid measures, designed to measure liquid ingredients, are clear plastic or glass pitchers marked with measurements on the sides.

MEASURING SPOONS

Metal (my preference) or plastic, these come in sets of ¼, ½, and 1 teaspoon plus 1 tablespoon; some sets also include ⅛-teaspoon and 1½-tablespoon measures. It is helpful to know that 3 teaspoons equal 1 tablespoon.

MICROWAVE OVEN

A microwave is good for reheating sauces, liquefying crystallized honey, melting butter, heating small quantities of liquid, and bringing ingredients such as milk, cream, or butter to room temperature (very, very carefully!). Use it to thaw frozen ingredients or make rock-hard ice cream scoopable. See page 98 for how to melt chocolate in a microwave.

MIXERS

For the recipes in this collection, it is nice to have a stand mixer, but a handheld mixer will do all jobs. If you have both type of mixers but prefer not to haul out the big one for every little thing, save it for the meringues and pavlova.

PANCAKE TURNER

Removing individual cookies from baking sheets is easiest to do with an ordinary pancake turner/spatula. Choose the thin metal kind; plastic or nonstick ones are thicker and harder to slip under cookies.

PARCHMENT AND WAX PAPER

Parchment paper is more reliable than butter or oil on the bottom of cake pans, and it is often my liner of choice on cookie sheets too. Precut parchment paper sheets are easier to use than pieces torn from a roll. Sheets are available from King Arthur Flour (see Resources, page 277). Wax paper is cheaper than parchment and useful for tasks that do not require the special characteristics of parchment, such as providing a landing place for sifted flour or chocolate-dipped strawberries, or for separating layers of cookies, etc.

SCALE

Electronic scales that register in decimals or fractions are inexpensive and easy to use. Weights in my recipes are also given in decimals. If your scale registers fractions, see the chart on page 288 to convert decimals to fractions. In most cases, for convenience, I have rounded weights to increments of 0.125 (or ⅛ ounce).

SILICONE SPATULAS AND WOODEN SPOONS

For cooking stovetop custards, puddings, and sauces, wooden spoons are okay, but heatproof silicone spatulas are even better at sweeping the sides, bottom, and corners of a pan without missing a square inch of territory—and they are better at scraping all of the contents from the pan into another container. The best silicone spatulas do not have detachable handles, which may come apart unexpectedly. It's nice to have at least one very large and one regular-size spatula.

STRAINERS

A large medium-fine strainer sifts flour and other dry ingredients perfectly, requires only one hand, and shakes out and cleans more easily than a sifter. The same strainer, or one even finer, is good for straining custards, as well as for removing the seeds from berry purees. Fine-mesh strainers (or even a little tea strainer) are best for dusting desserts with powdered sugar or cocoa.

TART PANS

Round tart pans with fluted edges and removable bottoms come in many sizes, but for this book you need only a 9½-inch pan. Choose shiny reflective pans rather than those made of darkened steel.

THERMOMETERS

Ovens that are too hot or too cool are not such a big deal for most cooking, but cakes and cookies suffer in ovens that run hot or cool. Oven thermometers are inexpensive and useful for checking the accuracy of your oven dial. An instant-read thermometer is useful for making sure that custards and other egg mixtures are adequately hot.

TIMER

A timer keeps the busy cook from forgetting what's in the oven before it's too late.

WHISKS

Wire whisks are great not only for blending batters and whipping cream but also for blending

dry ingredients together and fluffing up flour in lieu of sifting.

ZESTER

A Microplane zester removes the colored top layer of citrus peels, transforming it into the thinnest shreds effortlessly and without any bitter white pith (or scraped knuckles). I also use a Microplane for grating nutmeg and cinnamon sticks.

RESOURCES

BOBA TEA DIRECT

www.bobateadirect.com

A good source for Thai tea leaves.

INDIA TREE

1421 Elliott Avenue

Seattle, WA 98119

800-369-4848; 206-270-0293

www.indiatree.com

A great resource for spices and for muscovado sugar. Their products are available in specialty stores and better supermarkets, but you can also order them online.

KING ARTHUR FLOUR

The Baker's Catalogue

PO Box 876

Norwich, VT 05055-0876

800-827-6836

www.kingarthurflour.com

Everything for the baker and dessert maker, including cake and tart pans, kitchen utensils, and precut parchment sheets as well as cocoa, specialty sugars, vanilla beans, and more.

PARRISH'S CAKE DECORATING SUPPLY, INC.

225 West 146th Street

Gardena, CA 90248

800-736-8443

www.parrishsmagicline.com

A comprehensive source of ingredients and equipment for dessert makers.

THE PASTA SHOP

5655 College Avenue

Oakland, CA 94618

888-952-4005

www.rockridgemarkethall.com

A fabulous gourmet store with a second location in Berkeley. The buyers and owners solicit advice from an impressive list of local cookbook authors and professional bakers, so the store has a sub-specialty in baking ingredients and chocolate, including chocolate and cocoa from Scharffen Berger, Valrhona, Callebaut, E. Guittard, and Michel Cluizel; Madagascar and Tahitian vanilla extracts and whole and ground vanilla beans; honeys; nut pastes; specialty sugars; preserves; crystallized Australian ginger; and more.

PENZEY'S SPICES

PO Box 924

19300 West Janacek Court

Brookfield, WI 53008

800-741-7787

www.penzeys.com

All kinds of spices, including several types of cinnamon; crystallized Australian ginger; and Madagascar, Tahitian, and Mexican vanilla beans. Reading the catalog is an education in flavor ingredients and their uses.

SAINT GEORGE SPIRITS

2601 Monarch Street

Alameda, CA 94501

www.stgeorgespirits.com and www.hangarone.com

America's first and finest craft distiller makes exquisite Aqua Perfecta eaux de vie (framboise, kirsch, poire Williams, etc.) from local fruit.

SCHARFFEN BERGER CHOCOLATE MAKER

www.scharffenberger.com

Some of my favorite semisweet, bittersweet, extra-dark, unsweetened, and milk chocolates; limited-edition special chocolate blends; cacao nibs; and the best natural cocoa powder.

SUR LA TABLE

www.surlatable.com

A premium source for high-quality tools and equipment for home bakers and cooks; ingredients including Scharffen Berger, Valrhona, and E. Guittard chocolates.

THE VANILLA.COMPANY

www.vanilla.com

Superb vanilla, from beans to extracts, plus everything you've ever wanted to know about vanilla.

WHOLE FOODS

www.wholefoodsmarket.com

This upscale national natural food chain is a great source of natural and organic ingredients, including specialty flours and sugars; fine chocolates; bulk foods, including seeds, nuts, and grains; unsweetened shredded, dried, and flaked coconut; crystallized Australian ginger; and more.

DON'T FORGET LOCAL TREASURES

Health food and natural food stores and ethnic and high-end groceries, for bulk foods, grains, flours, seeds, spices, nuts, and inspiration.

Specialty coffee roasters and local cheese shops.

Restaurant supply stores, for equipment and utensils.

ACKNOWLEDGMENTS

It takes an entire cast to produce a book, and I am fortunate to work with the best players. At Artisan, my thanks to Peter Workman and to my very dear editor, Ann Bramson, as well as to Kevin Brainard, Trent Duffy, Bridget Heiking, Sibylle Kazeroid, Laurin Lucaire, Allison McGeehon, Nancy Murray, and Barbara Peragine. Maya Klein helped with recipe development and ideas; I am always grateful for her collaboration. Judith Sutton performed fierce (but wise) copyediting. Jennifer Morla designed yet another smart and beautiful book.

Art director and stylist Sara Slavin assembled the perfect photo team and offered the coveted (and so divine) Clyde Street Studio. Mark and Pierre welcomed us for two whole weeks, each in his own charming way. Photographer Sang An is a huge talent and dreamy to work with. Sandra Cook's food styling takes my breath away. And Penny Flood showed me how a kitchen on a shoot is *supposed* to run. Last and never least, I thank my agent and friend, Jane Dystel.

INDEX

CONVERSION CHARTS

Here are rounded-off equivalents between the metric system and the traditional systems that are used in the United States to measure weight and volume.

FRACTIONS / DECIMALS

FRACTIONS	DECIMALS
⅛	.125
¼	.25
⅓	.33
⅜	.375
½	.5
⅝	.625
⅔	.67
¾	.75
⅞	.875

WEIGHTS

US/UK	METRIC
¼ oz	7 g
½ oz	15 g
1 oz	30 g
2 oz	55 g
3 oz	85 g
4 oz	110 g
5 oz	140 g
6 oz	170 g
7 oz	200 g
8 oz (½ lb)	225 g
9 oz	250 g
10 oz	280 g
11 oz	310 g
12 oz	340 g
13 oz	370 g
14 oz	400 g
15 oz	425 g
16 oz (1 lb)	450 g

VOLUME

AMERICAN	IMPERIAL	METRIC
¼ tsp		1.25 ml
½ tsp		2.5 ml
1 tsp		5 ml
½ Tbsp (1½ tsp)		7.5 ml
1 Tbsp (3 tsp)		15 ml
¼ cup (4 Tbsp)	2 fl oz	60 ml
⅓ cup (5 Tbsp)	2½ fl oz	75 ml
½ cup (8 Tbsp)	4 fl oz	125 ml
⅔ cup (10 Tbsp)	5 fl oz	150 ml
¾ cup (12 Tbsp)	6 fl oz	175 ml
1 cup (16 Tbsp)	8 fl oz	250 ml
1¼ cups	10 fl oz	300 ml
1½ cups	12 fl oz	350 ml
2 cups (1 pint)	16 fl oz	500 ml
2½ cups	20 fl oz (1 pint)	625 ml
5 cups	40 fl oz (1 qt)	1.25 l

OVEN TEMPERATURES

	°F	°C	GAS MARK
very cool	250-275	130-140	½-1
cool	300	148	2
warm	325	163	3
moderate	350	177	4
moderately hot	375-400	190-204	5-6
hot	425	218	7
very hot	450-475	232-245	8-9